BY WAY OF

BEACHY HEAD

The story of a long walk

JOYCE TOMBS

PRAXIS BOOKS

Praxis Books
"Sheridan", Broomers Hill Lane, Pulborough,
West Sussex. RH20 2DU

ISBN 0 9528420 0 9

British Library Cataloguing–in–Publication Data.
A catalogue record for this book is available from
the British library.

Printed by Input Typesetting Ltd, Wimbledon.

This book is for the many who
made it possible.

CONTENTS

Introduction

When the typescript of this book arrived in my letter box, in spring 1996, I hadn't intended to take on another book for publication for many more months. But my very first glimpse of it aroused a sense of excitement and enjoyment, which has not abated since.

The idea of an elderly woman walking the length of England and Scotland is different, but not unique. Joyce is not the first person to have done it, nor the first to write about it. Perhaps that is the key to the charm of her story. She is no more or less special than the next person, and yet she drove herself on to achieve this goal. In her diaries, she records in plain language her experiences, the places she passed through, and in reading them we learn a very great deal.

We learn about an individual human spirit, putting one foot down in front of the other, and again and again...until she has walked 1000 miles. We learn about a lifelong marriage where the couple have shared a love of walking and wild places, mountains and solitude. We gain an insight into small irritations within the family which matter little in the wider picture. We glimpse Joyce's friends, who joined her for short sections of her walk, and find that she has a brisk and cheerful daughter. When she and Joyce disagree about the better route to take, they go separate ways, neither forcing her will onto the other.

At the same time, we see England and Scotland from the inside, away from the roads that so many of us are coming to loathe. We see our own homeland as it has always been, but from an angle which has become almost invisible. We see wonderful bed and breakfast hostesses, kind providers of tea and hot bathwater, tucked into the hills and villages and byways.

The simplicity of the writing somehow encourages the reader to look for metaphors. The walk itself – a uniquely individual choice of route, with its wrong turnings and surprises, both pleasant and unpleasant – can hardly fail to make us pause to think about how *we* would do it. And thereby we learn a little more about ourselves and our own approach to life. The highs and lows, the temptation to give up, the spells of nostalgia for past walks, the compulsion to plan for the coming days and ensure a safe resting place each night – all naturally lead us to thoughts of wider matters.

It is difficult to imagine anyone failing to find something to cherish in these pages. The geography itself has something for us all: a favourite spot in the Peaks or Pennines, seen through Joyce's eyes and described with great skill; or an area new to her, such as the Cotswolds. And not least we have the reassurance of knowing that even an experienced walker gets lost and tired and falls into peaty bogs.

Becky Smith. Autumn 1996

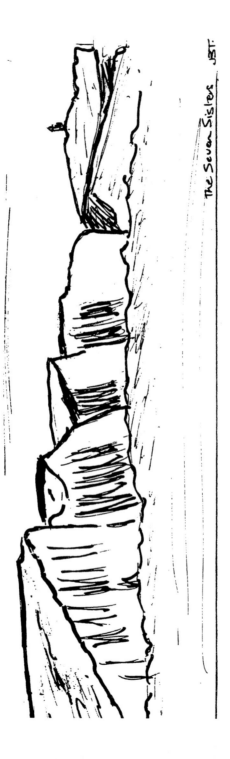

The Seven Sisters

JBT.

1: Endings and Beginnings

they tried to persuade me not to cross
the curious hills, finally shrugging
called me foolish, stubborn
that's how it is, I said, I'm going
where my pig is headed.

[anon]

When I arrived in Bath somebody asked me the question, 'Where is Beachy Head?' I had until then taken it for granted that everyone knows that Beachy Head is a chalk cliff on the south coast of England, most often in the news when someone drives a car over it. Beachy Head, I had assumed, would be as familiar to most people as would be the names of Nelson's Column or Windsor Castle.

It was a kind of measure of distance therefore to be asked about where I had come from. In Winchester to have walked from Beachy Head was common–place; in Bath it was something else, and I found myself struggling to give a sensible answer to the question. When I am doing a long–distance walk it isn't where I've come from that matters; somehow as the miles fall away behind me they also disappear, it's as if they've never been. What matters to me is where I am going tomorrow and the day after. Yesterday was history and could be forgotten for a time, and Beachy Head seemed to me like another country, like Australia, from whence my questioner hailed.

When I decided to do an end–to–end walk this notion of distance wasn't at all real. There was a starting point and a

1

finishing point and I had little concept of the miles to be covered and territory to be gained in between. It must be something about the defences we erect against our doubts and fears that does this, giving a goal to be achieved, but failing to spell out in any detail the magnitude of the task. In my case, once embarked upon a journey, as I walk I concentrate on the next mile, the next meal, the next night's lodging, and so on. Sufficient unto the day is the evil thereof was never said more appropriately.

I think the idea of doing a long walk had been incubating for a long time, perhaps for most of my sixty-five years. I had always loved hills and open spaces in spite of a childhood spent in a seaside town where the surrounding country was entirely horizontal for miles stretching inland from flat acres of sand. The only high points were sand dunes and railway bridges and I remember as a small child climbing the sliding slopes of the dunes because I could see further from there.

There seems never to have been a time when my deepest pleasure has not been found in the outdoors, and long-distance walking is a particular love, especially the kind which involves moving farther and farther from a starting point rather than walking in a circle to come back to it. Doing a walking trip is a way of shedding responsibilities if only for a few days, and of becoming detached from the day-to-day business of living. In coping with physical fatigue, weather, and terrain, the problems of living in an urban environment and being dependent on its many modern conveniences become increasingly irrelevant. Dishwashers and television sets have no place in the Scottish wilderness.

For most people, the opportunity for personal adventure has to take second place to demands of work and family, and there are few life stages when the freedom to do as one wishes is there, but retirement is one such time. So it was perhaps natural that when the time came to retire from a satisfying and demanding job I should think about long walks as a way of spending some of my new-found leisure.

In a career spanning fifty years I had never found growing older to offer any serious obstacles to doing things I wanted to do. The prospect of a third age seemed less an end than a beginning, offering different but no less rewarding opportunities. It was while talking with friends about what these might be that I announced that I was going to do a really long walk, from south to north of the British Isles.

I think I was rather alarmed by the way people responded. No one thought it at all odd for me to want to take off from end to end, or if they did think it odd they didn't say so; no one asked kindly if I didn't think I was too old for that sort of thing; it was just 'Oh what a good idea, I wish I could do that.' I took a step backward, so to speak, went home and did some hard thinking.

When some while later I said, 'Dick, I've decided I want to do an end-to-end walk', my husband's response was simply to ask when would I start and which route would I take. Gradually an awareness grew of the magnitude of the task I had set myself. The idea, in its infancy, had to be made real, to grow to maturity by way of lines on maps, estimates of distances to be walked, hills to be climbed; there were questions about where would I stay, what would I carry with me, how would I eat. Between the here and now and the time when I would start my walk rose a barrier seeming of Himalayan proportions which I should need to surmount before setting out.

I remained undeterred by the thought of obstacles which might lie ahead and in the final months of work I kept the notion somewhere at the back of my consciousness to be taken out and nurtured from time to time. From this a kind of plan emerged.

I made some decisions: the first one was that I didn't really want to start the walk from Land's End; I know most end-to-enders use it as a starting or finishing point, but when I looked in my atlas I began to wonder why. It isn't the most southerly point of mainland Britain; the Lizard Point a few miles east of Land's End bears that distinction. Even if Ireland is left out it isn't the most westerly either. Ardnamurchan Point in the western highlands of Scotland is *much* further west. Relieved of any nagging feeling that I should follow a well-trodden end-to-end trail, I made my own choice. I would find somewhere closer to home, just a few miles down the road on the Sussex coast.

My chosen starting-point, Beachy Head, is scenically dramatic enough, its chalk cliffs seeming as emblematic of England as are the cliffs of Dover. The clean cut made by the vertical drop to the sea tells as few sights can that Britain has boundaries formed by the action of the elements. If you turn your back to the sea at Beachy Head the whole countryside of the British Isles around three quadrants of the compass is open to you by way of a wealth of paths and trackways, ancient and modern.

At the other end, Duncansby Head at the north–east tip of Scotland, is further north than John o' Groats, but my motives for selecting Cape Wrath, in the North–West of Sutherland, for a finishing point, were different. Cape Wrath has some of the highest sea cliffs in the British Isles, and looks out over thous- ands of miles of ocean. To the north the next land is the frozen wastes of the Arctic, to the west the continent of America. Cape Wrath is set in wild and unyielding country with unpredictable weather. To get there on foot would mean miles of trackless walking and would need self–sufficiency and competence. If I managed the intervening miles Cape Wrath would be a fit place to end the walk.

I wanted to avoid walking on roads as much as possible, so I would plan my route along long–distance footpaths and trails. I bought a large–scale map of England, Wales and Scotland and drew some lines on it between Beachy Head and Cape Wrath. This made me realise how crooked the British Isles are; an enterprising bee aiming for Cape Wrath from Beachy Head would risk death by pollution in crossing Greater London and by drowning in the waters of the Firth of Forth; it would in the intervening miles cross the Pennines somewhere near Skipton after surviving the hazards of the East Midland coalfield. This bee, arriving exhausted but triumphant at Cape Wrath, would have flown a distance of about eight hundred miles.

My final route, after much puzzling over the problems of linking together a number of recognised footpaths with some of my own devising, looked more like the wanderings of a demen- ted ant, weaving its course through the populated southeast by way of the South Downs Way, turning north at Bath to scurry along the Cotswold Way, then bravely aiming for the narrow gap which divides the conurbations of Birmingham and Coventry. It would cross the flight of the bee somewhere in North Yorkshire,

4

when its line would be more directly north. Beyond the Scottish Borders, tracing the progress of the ant on the ground would look even more erratic, a succession of twists and turns which sometimes would leave it moving away from Cape Wrath rather than towards it. This ant by the time it arrived at Cape Wrath would have walked about two hundred and fifty miles further than the bee had flown.

End–to–end walkers have to make their own rules; they don't have to be many, but once made cheating isn't allowed. The most important rule of course, is that every step of the way has to be on one's own two feet. Even this rule went by the board when I realised that there would be times when a short boat trip would save many hours of walking round the head of one or two Scottish lochs. So my rule one turned out to be that I would walk every step of the way except when it seemed sensible to take a ferry. If I needed to go off route for food or accommodation I would use whatever transport was available, but would return each time to the point at which I had left off.

I spent some time wondering about how much help to accept in the way of company on the walk. There was a part of me that wanted to do it all by myself but I also knew that I was going to need support and encouragement; I expected that there would be low points when I would wonder if it was all worth it and at these times the knowledge that someone had confidence in me would make all the difference. I became aware too that the concept of the walk fired the imagination of my friends and family and in some ways they wanted to be part of it. So in the end I accepted help gratefully when it was offered. I am aware now how important this help was in enabling me to complete the walk, especially in its later stages, when I wasn't sure if I would last out to the end.

I decided I wasn't going to be a purist; where there seemed to be a more direct route than the guidebook said I would take it. I started to work it out in detail using maps, guides and literature. I also set a date for the start of the walk: Mayday 1991, not long after my sixty–eighth birthday. This seemed a long way ahead, but there were other things to do; I needed to give myself time to disengage from the working world so that I could concentrate on this next challenge.

One question most asked of people who set out on journeys like mine is 'Why are you doing this?'. It's always possible to rationalise about motives. Many people collect money for charities, as if getting something tangible out of it provides some kind of justification for what might seem a pointless way to spend one's time. There must be more to it than that, though, easier ways to collect money or to see new places; T.S. Eliot said it best:

> the end of all our exploring
> will be to arrive where we started
> and know the place for the first time.

Since self–knowledge is unique to the individual, I think the only honest reply to the question 'Why do you do it?' is 'I don't know, but I'm doing this to find out.'

By the autumn of 1990 I had the route just about worked out. The next stage was to plan the details of equipment, and organise my support parties. Time seemed to go by quickly, with so many things happening in the outside world. I continued with plans, and as 1991 approached, became increasingly impatient to go and oddly fearful that in some way I might be prevented from going. Crises in international affairs, and especially the West's involvement in war in the Gulf, added to the uncertainty I was feeling.

Early in 1991 I felt pangs of sadness in reading of the death of Alfred Wainwright, whose writings inspired so many long–distance walkers. I took out my copy of *Pennine Way Companion*, stained and dogeared from its treatment on my Pennine Way walk (the first long–distance walk I had ever done), and thought of how I had at first felt irritated with AW's style, rather impatient at his jokes, and how over the miles this had been replaced by affection and respect for the genuineness of AW's feeling for the countryside and ability to transfer his vast knowledge to paper. If I had to write an epitaph for AW it would be from his introduction to *Pennine Way Companion*: 'The walk will do you good'. I hope he understood how true this was for the many people who followed in his footsteps.

I had worked out a schedule of how to spend my time until Mayday. My training for another London Marathon was well advanced, and would take my mind off my impatience to be off. After the marathon, on April 21st, I would have some intensive last minute preparations to do before my departure on May 1st.

Late in February disaster struck. Out on a training run I had a sudden agonising pain in my right ankle. This had always been a weak spot after an injury many years ago, but I expected that a few days' rest would put it right. Three weeks later I was still hobbling about, unable even to jog a few steps. The sympathetic osteopath whom I saw diagnosed a torn tendon, advised rest, and said that such injuries took around four months to heal; running was out of the question. I was a non-starter for the London Marathon and could only hope that with rest and treatment I would be sufficiently fit to start the walk.

Frustrated beyond belief I continued my preparation hoping desperately that this wouldn't put a total stop to the expedition. By the end of April the tendon was healed but the joint had stiffened and I was having a lot of pain just walking. I put back my departure date to May 22nd, which was about as late as I could reasonably hope to leave.

I began to think seriously about the wisdom of starting the walk at all, with the added handicap of a stiff ankle. The alternative, of putting off the walk for another year, seemed unthinkable. I had already invested so much in the project that I felt I would rather start off, and if completing the whole route in one go turned out to be impossible I would break off at that point and complete it next year. Having made that decision I felt better and waited for the day of departure. I had waited as long as possible to decide where I would make my overnight stops in the first few days of the walk, and I remember spending an afternoon making telephone calls and being reluctant to pick up the receiver, feeling that I was about to commit myself to something where the outcome was uncertain, and wondering if I would really be able to keep to the stages I had set myself.

After all the soul-searching packing was an anti-climax; using lists accumulated over the years I gathered the gear together. There were the essentials like maps, guidebooks, compass, waterproofs, survival blanket, change of clothes, spare socks, a light sweater, hat and gloves (because even on the South Downs in May it has been known to snow!). I added light slippers for the evenings, and a lightweight nightdress, not essential but more comfortable. To all this had to be added first aid gear, plasters, bandages, insect repellant, a few aspirin tablets, washing things and comb, scissors, sewing things, spare spectacles and a small torch. There there were documents: an exercise book for my diary, accommodation lists, B&B book and route instructions I had prepared for myself; cheque book, credit cards, money and YHA card. I would need four maps to take me to Salisbury, where I would meet Dick, but could post maps home as I covered the ground, so I would need envelopes and stamps. A book was a must, and after searching the shelves I chose Tolkien's *Lord of the Rings* as embodying a quest of another kind. My camera and spare film I would carry separately in a small waist pouch. I added a small water bottle and a lunchbox with some iron rations: raisins, chocolate, glucose. I could buy food for lunches as I went along. My final item, a small radio, was pure luxury, but why not?

I don't think I bothered to weigh my Karrimor rucksack when all this had been packed. I simply lifted it and tested the weight, which I guessed to be something between twelve and fifteen pounds. We had decided long ago that this was the optimum comfortable weight for a backpacking trip; any more becomes burdensome. The familiarities of the operation made the prospect of setting out less formidable. All that was left was to wait for tomorrow.

2: Ghosts on the Downs

I will go out against the sun
Where the rolled scarp retires,
And the Long Man of Wilmington
Looks naked toward the shires.

[Kipling]

When in the 1950s I came from Derbyshire to live and work in London I was convinced that there was no walking worth doing south and east of a line drawn from the Bristol Channel diagonally across England to somewhere near Hull. At every opportunity I would retreat across that magic line, first for weekends in the Peak District and later for climbing trips to North Wales; so it took me a long time to discover the South Downs.

I can't quite remember when it was that somebody took me for a walk from Amberley station up the steep hill on to Amberley Mount, along the broad ridges of Sullington and Chantry Hills then down to cross the gap where the road rushes to the coast through Washington, and on up the stony chalk track past a quarry and so to Chanctonbury Ring. I at once recognised it as my kind of country, finding in the smooth slopes and long views the same sense of space that I identified with the Derbyshire moors, where I had first learned about walking. To find the South Downs so close to the crowded cities of the south seemed nothing short of miraculous, and the knowledge that they were there offered comfort on dreary days when I longed to escape from the London suburbs.

It was my feeling for the South Downs that made Beachy

9

SOUTH DOWNS WAY
Part I

Bignor Houghton Ashington Chantonbury Ring

Steyning

EAST

WEST
SUSSEX

Rodmell SUSSEX

Alfriston

Littlehampton Worthing Brighton Newhaven Eastbourne

Beachy
Head

Head the right place for me to start my adventure. So familiar, it would be almost like stepping out of my own front door into my own garden and going on from there; not at first having to think too much about route–finding or getting lost or being in wild and lonely country where if things went wrong there would be no one to turn to. I needed to have the reassurance that came from knowing where I was and where I was going and from seeing views and places that I had seen many times before. After the South Downs – well, I'd think about that when I came to it.

Wednesday 22nd May 1991: It was such a relief to be there at last, on Beachy Head with rucksack, crooked stick and camera, ready to go. It was a fine May morning, warm sun and fluffy white clouds, just the day to start a long walk.

Dick had taken me by car to our local station; a quick goodbye, and I was boarding the suburban train I had so often taken before. The familiar action of taking the train added to the sense of unreality I was feeling.

On the station at East Croydon, where I waited for the main line train to Eastbourne, I saw an ex–colleague whom I knew only slightly and who certainly had never seen me with boots and rucksack. I didn't want to have to explain myself, so crept into the waiting room to avoid her, and was glad when the train arrived and I could sneak into a different compartment.

The carriage was full of day trippers, mostly of about my vintage. I tried to read the *Guardian*, full of news about savage dog legislation, couldn't take in what I was reading, and in the end gave up and sat watching through the window for the first sight of the South Downs. It came, a view of the long green hillside above Alfriston, and, eager to be off, I waited for the train to draw into Eastbourne station.

The taxi set me down outside the Beachy Head Hotel. Such a familiar place, people strolling around in the spring sunshine, the grassy slopes across the road stretching away to the cliff–top and, five hundred feet below, the calm sea. Conscious of how the weight of my rucksack was bearing down on my stiff ankle, I walked carefully across the road, over the green turf to the viewpoint, my chosen spot for the start of the walk. I found a likely–looking person, a young man, to take my photograph for the record, relieved that he didn't ask any questions about why and where.

The story is told of how the martyred St Denis carried his head over two leagues from Paris to his home village; it is of this mythical feat that French author Mme de Deffaud wrote: 'the distance is nothing; it is only the first step that is difficult'. I wondered how true that was for me as with my head firmly on my shoulders (or so I hoped), I took that step and then another and another, and set off for Birmingham. If Chesterton had chosen Birmingham as a place to go to, so could I, I thought; it certainly felt closer than Cape Wrath. Once I'd reached Birmingham would be time enough to think about where I was going next. It was 12.45pm. There was a dreamlike quality about leaving the workaday world for my own excursion into other times, other places. This was the day that Rajiv Gandhi was assassinated. Oil wells were burning in Kuwait, people were suffering from the aftermath of a war in Iraq; in our own country children were being abused and people sleeping in the streets. All this became for me irrelevant as if a glass screen had descended between me and the outside world.

The first thing that happened of course was that I fell down! Well, perhaps not quite the first thing. I'd passed Belle Tout Lighthouse and was on the summit of the hill before descending to Birling Gap. My foot gave way and the weight of the rucksack pulled me over. I got up quickly, looking around to make sure no one had seen me fall and feeling foolish, relieved that I seemed to have suffered no injury.

Walking more carefully I descended to Birling Gap for coffee then set off to tackle the Seven Sisters, the line of shining chalk cliffs that follow a switchback course westwards to descend to the sea at Cuckmere Haven. It was a perfect afternoon, the sea calm at high tide, the downs covered in wild flowers, heartsease, cowparsley, bugle, and distant fields brilliant with rape. Sheep were cropping the sweet grass and there were rabbits everywhere. After leaving the road and carpark I seemed to have the Downs to myself.

I sat in the sun to eat late lunch, watching the seabirds flying below me and listening to the skylarks. It was here that I first felt that I was really on my way; my confidence had been sorely tested as a result of my injury, and throughout the past weeks I had often doubted that I would be fit enough to begin my walk. Once I had decided to start the rest seemed just a matter of carrying out plans already made. Walking after all is easy; you just put one foot in front of another and keep doing it. So I told myself as one after the other each hill in its turn fell away behind me: Went Hill Brow, Baily's Brow, Flagstaff Point, Brass Point, Rough Brow, Short Brow, and Haven Brow. I descended the slope of the Downs and walked along the Cuckmere River to Alfriston, with swans on the water and evening drawing on.

May 23rd: The South Downs Way follows the chalk ridge from Eastbourne to Winchester, descending to sea level only at points where rivers cut through the escarpment, so there are long stretches where there are no dwellings and it is possible to feel a sense of isolation even in the overcrowded southeast. Alfriston is by way of being a honey-pot for motorists and day trippers, but once out of the village I climbed on to the escarpment to follow the stony track for about six miles before descending to the river Ouse at Southease. My destination for the night was the village of Rodmell, about two miles further on.

For the rest of the South Downs Way I was to be accompanied by friendly ghosts from times past. There are many ways of covering the distance along the ridge: on foot, on horseback, or by bicycle. All my excursions had been on foot, mostly on challenge walks requiring a fixed route to be followed within a given time limit: a hundred, eighty, or twenty-six miles. I thus had memories of companionship and shared joys and hardships which were to imbue the whole of the South Downs Way with a special significance The most vivid memories are of night walks, when even the most well-walked path changes into something strange and unfamiliar, and the lights along the coast appear to belong to an alien world. It is easy to go astray at such times, and there is reassurance and pleasure in the presence of walking companions. Now on a summer morning the tracks were comfortingly familiar, and I had plenty of time to look around me and to relish the long views.

After leaving the main track at the summit of the hill outside Alfriston the route crosses cereal fields to reach the car park at Bostal Hill, a favourite spot for hang–gliders. Today the sun was shining and the north–east wind was blowing gently to my rear, but I had been here in less benign conditions, in fierce wind and low temperatures. The barn on the hill bears witness to the storm of October 1987 which blew its roof away.

Beyond Bostal Hill the ploughed fields give way to a grassy track and sheep grazing. This is a beautiful section of the route, with views to the distant sea on one side and across the Weald on the other; the track stretches invitingly ahead, cowslips, birdseye, and white campion growing in profusion. It was here that I met my first wayfarers, a couple on the last day of their trek from Buriton to Eastbourne.

At the farm at Southease a farmhand called out, 'I like your crooked stick.' I laughed, and looked at my stick with affection. It had been made for me by Dick out of a stake from the cherry tree in our own garden, crooked because it had grown that way. I had carried my crooked stick on many journeys, and loved it for its imperfections as one loves an old friend. Another walker was filling a water–bottle at the tap in the farmyard. Hearing that he was about to finish his journey brought home to me for the first time how far I had to go; even Winchester seemed too distant and, feeling so aware how slowly I was going I didn't dare say that I was on an end–to–end walk. I had deliberately chosen to start with two short days to stretch my walking legs but felt rather like a snail crawling across the map.

I had time to spare today so sat outside the little round-towered Norman church at Southease to eat my sandwiches before continuing along the road to Rodmell thinking what a pity it is that the South Downs Way has such sections where heavy traffic takes away the pleasure of walking. I wandered through the village, passing Monk House, where Virginia Woolf had lived, and came to my night's lodging, where, turning on the news I learned of Rajiv Gandhi's assassination.

May 24th: In the small hours I lay awake wondering if I had been foolish to start the walk at all. I don't think I had ever felt so alone; my ankle was stiff and painful, and after an hour or so's walking my back started to hurt. I faced the prospect of having to cope with the pain for the next ten weeks and asked myself if it was really worth it. I was still near enough to home for the prospect of being there to seem appealing, without the necessity for persisting with what now seemed a futile enterprise. I could get a bus down the road the three miles to Lewes, catch a fast train, and be home within two hours.

The idea seemed enormously attractive, and I considered going home just for the weekend. This would do no harm since Dick was away in Lancashire and I would be able to come back and continue the walk without anyone knowing. I fell asleep thinking that this was what I might do, only to realise on waking that this was one of those dark hour proposals which don't stand the impact of daylight. Whatever the suffering of going on, it would have been nothing compared to the disgrace of having to confess defeat at this early stage of the walk. The only way to go was on, and it was that realisation which set me off next morning. It was going to be a long day, with about twice the previous day's mileage to cover.

Feeling better I set off up Mill Lane, to join my friendly ghosts on a familiar and loved section. The may was in full and fragrant bloom and the verges full of cow parsley; I looked out to the left to Seaford Head above Cuckmere, still only a day's walk away. A fell-runner passed me coming in the opposite direction, then there was total peace, difficult to realise that down on the coast people were preparing for an influx of Bank Holiday visitors.

It had turned colder, the wind round to the South-east, and there was a sea wrack in the air, but I made good progress on to open country through farmland then on to grassy downland and the escarpment overlooking Lewes, passing the two dewponds which provide welcome landmarks, especially to those walking on the Downs in mist or darkness. The first one has been restored by a conservation group, the litter and detritus of years having been removed.

Passing walkers setting off up the track with packs heavy with camping equipment, I descended to the Newmarket Inn on the stroke of noon, for coffee and a sandwich and a three-quarter hour halt. I crossed the busy A27 road, nearly getting mown down by a lorry and went straight up the hill on the other side, into woods and seeing game birds and wood anemones. What a long way it seemed up to the South Downs Way under Black Cap, where the route turns west after swinging north to avoid the built up coastal towns. I said a less than regretful farewell to Seaford Head disappearing to the rear, and felt that at last I was making progress.

I visited the trig point of Ditchling Beacon, at 813 feet the high point of the South Downs Way, it remaining cold enough for gloves and hat. Then, feeling weak, I stopped to eat the remains of my lunchtime sandwich. Surprisingly soon I was descending past the windmills Jack and Jill to Pyecombe, and a really horrendous crossing of road construction where the new Brighton by–pass was being built. I was glad to climb out of sight and earshot over the final hill to Saddlescombe. After a long day my damaged ankle protested strongly as I descended the steep slope to the road and left the South Downs Way to follow a path through woods to Manor Farm at Poynings. I went to bed feeling happier about my progress, as I seemed to have survived the longest day up to now, and felt more optimistic about tackling tomorrow's stage, which would be equally long.

May 25th: Saturday. The day promised to be hot, and before I had gone half a mile from Manor Farm I was stopping to discard jacket and put on my sun hat. The farmer had directed me back to the South Downs Way without having to retrace my steps from the previous evening. This was an interesting and spectac- ular route, taking me on an ascending contouring path along the side of the Devil's Dyke. The Dyke is a deep trench carved out of the downs, an attempt by the Devil to flood the Weald and its churches it is said. The Devil was foiled by a false dawn created by a candle, so fled before the task was completed.

I climbed steeply out of the Dyke to rejoin the ridge, almost falling on to the path, not having seen the step, to the consternation of a passing walker. Back on route, it became busy; I soon met a large school party, followed in quick succession by a pack of beagles taking three huntsmen in red jackets out for a walk; pause for photographs.

I started having a conversation with myself of the kind which was to become habitual over the coming weeks; in solo walking you don't have anyone to talk to about how you are feeling, how far it is, where to stop for the next rest, which of the paths in front of you to take. All the decisions are yours to make, and I would be constantly consulting myself about distances, times, my forward plans, and whether to keep to the route I had worked out or try something else. This kind of inner dialogue kept me from thinking too much about the state of my ankle, or, if that was not hurting, my backache.

Today the argument was about whether I should keep to the South Downs Way or descend into Steyning for a short cut and, incidentally, lunch. After an unexpected find of a coffee halt at Summerdene Farm, it was the South Downs Way that won, so I crossed the river Adur and its water meadows to the little village of Botolph's and toiled up the hill on the other side then found a spot in a cornfield to eat lunch in perfect peace, reflecting on how much I was enjoying my own company. It was hard to remember that only thirty-six hours earlier I had considered abandoning the walk

More traffic came along, a group of young women who plaintively asked how far to Eastbourne; cyclists on brightly coloured mountain bikes; hang-gliders in the distance looking like fantastic multi-coloured birds; and two loaded back-packers going my way. Feeling the effect of yesterday's exertions I limped along to poor mutilated Chanctonbury Ring, devastated in the storm of 1987. I had wept when I first saw how the silhouette of the downs had changed. From afar the ring of beech trees appears intact, but it is only from closer at hand that the full extent of the devastation is revealed, just an outer fringe of trees remaining. I tried to imagine what it must have been like to be on the ridge of the downs in that great storm.

It being a bank holiday weekend I had had problems with accommodation and had eventually booked a bed at Ashington, some way off route to the north. I'd hoped to go there by bus, but it turned out that there wasn't one. I felt that I had already done enough walking for one day, but there was nothing for it but to continue on foot.

I set off along leafy lanes, bordered with more wild flowers, the trees arching overhead and the birds beginning their even-song. I moved away from the ridge of the Downs then climbed again, a long hill to reach the little village church at Warmington; dusk was falling and an owl called from a yew tree.

Ashington is a characterless place bisected by the main A24 road. Light-headed with fatigue I racked my brains to remember the instructions I had been given to locate my night's lodging, and failed to make any sense of them. I wandered around a housing estate knocking on doors, then to my relief found a village store where the owner was just shutting up shop, but was able to direct me to the house aptly named Sunbeams, a lovely place set in gardens full of summer flowers.

Felicity, aptly named too, greeted me as if I was a cherished elderly relative, offering me tea, bath, and food, in quick succession, talking non-stop the while. Felicity clearly had a talent for looking after people and divided her attention between me and an airline pilot husband. Kept company by Felicity's four cats, I ate voraciously of home-made oxtail soup and an enormous salad, retiring to a sybaritically comfortable bed to watch 'Casualty' on the mini-television. The walk was already becoming memorable for the kindness and generosity of the people I met, and the night's stay stands out as an oasis.

May 26th: I gratefully accepted a lift with Felicity to rejoin my route next morning at Washington. Back on the ridge the skylarks were shouting their heads off on a grey misty morning, with a gentle following wind. Traffic was brisk on this Sunday morning: cyclists, runners, walkers, a horse, and the same two backpackers I'd seen at Chanctonbury last evening. With all the people about, there was still the sense of space with the Weald stretching away on the one side and a glimpse of sea on the other, then the view of the Arun River meandering across the Amberley plain. This section of the Way is rich in prehistoric remains, tumuli all around Rackham Hill, and a field system thousands of years old. I descended to Amberley station, deciding there that I deserved an afternoon off after walking more than forty miles in two and a half days.

Amberley and Houghton have many attractions: a castle, a

museum, a pub, and a riverside cafe. I headed for the latter, to drink coffee, to telephone ahead for accommodation, and to eat lunch by the river Arun. It had turned warm and there were many family parties at the long tables, each in its exclusive small group, children feeding the chaffinches, cyclists, walkers, and boating parties on the river, just the way to spend a holiday afternoon. It was good to have no immediate need to get up and go. Locked into my own dimension I felt immensely refreshed, cocooned from all the preoccupations of everyday life, with demands made on me only the self-imposed ones. I realised that I was more than halfway to Winchester.

I finally wandered along the road to Houghton, where I had booked for the night, diving into the hedge from time to time to avoid getting mown down by fast traffic. I felt aggrieved that walkers were not allowed for at all on this busy road, and wondered why no one had tried to route the South Downs Way along the river (this became clear later; doing an evening walk I discovered that all the riverside land was in the estate of the Duke of Norfolk who obviously didn't welcome the public on to his property.[1]

May 27th: Bank Holiday Monday. I breakfasted with two walkers doing the SDW in the opposite direction, and complaining of sore feet. I felt smug about my lack of blisters (in fact throughout the walk I had no such problem) and began to feel more optimistic about my own chances. I had crossed the last major river on the South Downs Way, and from now on would be heading for the Bristol Channel. I had walked across two maps and two counties and by tomorrow I would be in Hampshire.

It was a fine morning, the north wind blowing away the murk. I toiled uphill between verges of pink campion, seeing magpies and enough swallows to make a summer, but the skylarks

---

[1]Measures are being taken to make the South Downs Way less hazardous by avoiding dangerous main roads, for example Rodmell is to be by-passed, and a new footbridge has been opened over the River Arun between Amberley and Bury.

seemed to have gone. It felt at first like climbing Everest, one breath to a step uphill, and it was a relief to be on more level ground. I came to Bignor Hill, which was occupied by picnic parties, and joined a Roman road.

It is seldom possible to journey far in Britain without coming across traces of Roman occupation. I had already passed the site of a Roman temple built on the remains of an even older Iron Age fort in the centre of what is now Chanctonbury Ring. Here now was Stane Street, built, curiously enough, as a relief road to supplement Watling Street, to take the legions from the coast to London . It seems that even in those days there were problems with traffic congestion.

Watling Street ran from Dover first to London then to the Welsh borders, while Stane Street linked London with the small ports known collectively as Chichester Harbours, driving a straight line across the Wealden clay to cross the North Downs at Tyrell's Wood near Box Hill. Like many Roman roads, Stane Street has been used by subsequent road builders, and can be traced by the long straight stretches of the A29 road between Dorking in Surrey and Billingshurst in West Sussex, where it leaves the tarmac to cross the South Downs.

A mile down Bignor Hill, off my route, are the remains of one of the biggest Roman houses in Roman Britain, thought to have been the residence of the governor of the province of Regum. My path however lay in another direction, saying only an *ave atque vale* to Stane Street which descends from Bignor Hill to head south–west to Chichester. The South Downs Way stays faithful to the crest of the downs, following the track over green sheep–cropped fields and through woods down to Littleton, then climbing again to Woolavington Down.

A tractor was working in the next field. The early mist had cleared to blue sky and fluffy white clouds and there was a splendid view back to the sweep of the Downs all the way round to Chanctonbury Ring. I was soon into thick woodland, only to emerge to a view of rolling Sussex countryside to the south, rich green fields and hills contrasting with the cropped chalk of the eastern Downs.

I turned off–route for a mile to Cocking, a small village

nestling below the downs, to a rambling bungalow set in rampantly flowering gardens. In these country settings gardens become a different concept entirely from those where vegetation struggles to survive against urban dirt and fumes in large towns. My friendly hostess gave me tea and home–made cake and talked about hazards of living in the country, of agricultural noise and pollution.

May 28th: I sent off my first completed film then followed my hostess's directions to find a peaceful bridleway climbing through beautiful old oak woods. I turned a corner to rejoin the South Downs Way on the summit of Cocking Down and exchanged greetings with a young backpacker resting there. He'd walked from Winchester yesterday, he said, and expected to reach Eastbourne, more than sixty miles distant, that evening.

I went on over open downland at first then through more old beech and oak woodland. I was seeing for the first time the devastation caused by the 1987 storm in this part of the Downs, but in this beautiful lush scenery the vegetation has grown to throw a blanket of green over mutilated stumps and exposed roots. Small clearings have been created to allow woodland flowers to grow, in a healing process which will, if allowed to happen naturally, result in a renewal of the countryside, different perhaps, but showing how growing things are capable of recovery if left to themselves.

The direct climb up Beacon Hill is dauntingly steep, and I chose to follow the South Downs Way along the route which skirts its flanks, longer but easier on wind and limb. Harting Down which follows is accessible by road so had the usual rash of parked cars and people walking their dogs. I went on into farmland, leaving West Sussex for Hampshire as I walked through beech woods to Sunwood Farm, then along a splendid avenue of copper beeches and a long descent to Buriton village.

Buriton is a really picture–postcard village; the church overlooks a pond with drifts of water–lilies and a weeping willow dipping its leaves into the water. I went to find my night's lodging at the Old Hop Kiln, conscious of having reached another mile marker. In two days I would be in Winchester, and leaving the comforting familiarity of the SDW for territory which was

SOUTH DOWNS WAY
Part II

HAMPSHIRE

Winchester

West Meon

Southampton

Buriton

WEST SUSSEX

Cocking

Bignor

Chichester

Portsmouth

Selsey

Bognor Regis

for me uncharted. I would not be in known country before reaching Derbyshire, and felt excited at the prospect of seeing the west country and the Cotswolds.

May 29th: The start of my second week's walking was inauspicious, a mixture of disaster and farce; though breakfast was lovely, served country–house style from a hotplate with the *Daily Telegraph* and all. I started back along the road to rejoin the South Downs Way as it goes through Queen Elizabeth country park, then decided to take a short cut on a small path leading into woods, which from the map looked as though it would cut off a corner. The path, ill–defined at first, became clearer, and I followed it deep into the woods beneath beech trees, climbing steadily, with the occasional waymark to reassure me that I was on a regular track.

I had been going, I suppose, a half hour, when I saw a figure ahead of me standing on the path near where it joined a wider track at a T–junction ahead. As I drew nearer I saw that it was a smallish man of indeterminate age, dressed in an odd–looking bright blue waterproof jacket which appeared not to fit him properly, with sleeves too long for his short arms. He had a round, chubby face, curiously lacking in expression. We exchanged greetings and, more for the sake of making conversation than for need of direction, asked if he knew which path led to the country park centre. He replied quite vaguely, that he didn't know. I was just turning away when, quite suddenly, he said, 'Will you do something for me?'

I looked back, and found him in the act of unzipping his jeans. My first reaction was disbelief, my second absolute fury, which quite eclipsed any fear I might be expected to have. I called out something like 'How dare you, bugger off', words which I would never have expected to use, and fled, disturbed, and angry with myself for being disturbed. I hurried on, turning downhill at the junction in my anxiety to get away and realising too late that I should have turned uphill. Unwilling to go back I went on knowing that I was moving away from my planned route.

The forest had become tainted for me, and I was thankful to come out of the trees and into fields. I crossed the main Portsmouth road near Petersfield in the middle of some truly horrific roadworks and revised my route to accommodate my new position. I continued down a minor road, resentfully convinced that my day was ruined.

It was fortunate that at that point another walker caught me up to talk about the butterfly survey he was doing, and we ambled along the road together, until he left to strike off into the hills and I continued into the pretty village of East Meon, feeling that on the whole the world was still a friendly place. I sat on the village green to eat my packed lunch and ruminate on the events of the morning. Things improved; I found a bridleway across the hillside through fields of lush grass with sheep and cows grazing, then descended to walk by the infant river Meon among the buttercups, my boots yellow with pollen.

I arrived early in West Meon to find my night's lodging, the Old Courthouse, beautifully set in a country garden, honeysuckle, roses and peonies in profusion, free range chickens roaming the grounds, unlocked doors but no one in. A friendly Alsatian appeared, disarming my natural suspicions of large dogs by bringing me stones to throw. I sat on the grass in hot sunshine thinking that this was about the most energetic occupation I needed at the time, until eventually a young woman, the daughter of my hostess I learned, hurried up with apologies and let me in. *May 30th:* The harsh cries of peacocks and cockcrow awoke me, not the kind of reveille usually met in towns; my hostess thought them a nuisance. This was a wonderful old house, some 14th century, with huge rooms, furniture in proportion. Must have needed enormous fires to heat all this space.

After walking across the field path to Warnford I was immensely encouraged by finding a signpost saying Winchester ten miles. I knew it was further by SDW, but still and all, by this evening I would have walked my first hundred miles. Feeling cheerful again I climbed on to Wheely Down, green grass against dark woods and on to Beacon Hill to regain the South Downs Way. I dropped into a roadside pub for morning coffee, feeling like an alien among crowds of lunching motorists.

I crossed the main road to Gander Down and sat under an oak tree to eat lunch, basking in the warm sunshine. Saying a good-bye to the South Downs Way, I then continued along green lanes to Temple Valley and Telegraph Hill. My blissful solitude was shattered when I descended towards the noise and fumes of the M3 motorway, mercifully skirting Winchester, but only with the loss of much beautiful countryside. I took a last look at lovely Twyford Down, doomed to be the next casualty sacrificed on the altar of the great god of motor transport.

I walked by the river into the centre of Winchester, conscious that I was well and truly back in civilisation after eight days of quiet villages. Tomorrow was to be my first rest day. One important milestone had been reached and it looked as though my planning of times and stages had been accurate. A rest day here would satisfactorily punctuate the walk.

It was good next day to do normal sorts of chores, washing shirt and socks, shopping, writing postcards, and some honest-to-goodness sight-seeing. I visited the cathedral and paid my respects to Jane Austen who is buried here, took photographs, sat by the river, and returned to the cathedral to hear the choir rehearsing evensong, then caught the bus back up the Stockbridge road, thankful that I didn't have to walk this uphill section twice.

Feeling restored and refreshed I set off for Salisbury and points west.

Bath

Trowbridge

WILTSHIRE

HAMPSHIRE

Warminster

Stockbridge

Houghton

Fovant   Salisbury   Winchester

Shaftesbury

Winchester to Bath

3: Take the road out west...

Saturday June 1st: From Winchester I was bound for Wiltshire, over chalk downland, descending to cross the river Test, then woods and farmland, finally the Clarendon estate to Salisbury, crossing the county boundary west of Stockbridge. Besides changes in the terrain I began to observe differences in how people talked; the nasal cockney accents and middle–class intonation of the south–east were giving way to broader vowels and slower speech. I became conscious of how outside the towns the pace of life had slowed, less traffic, fewer houses, fewer people. I was beginning to feel less anxious about the day–to–day organisation of the walk, more confident that things would work out.

I discovered that there is a twenty–six mile long Clarendon Way joining the two cathedral cities, Winchester and Salisbury which generally follows the line I had decided to take, and I came across its well–placed waymarks from time to time. First I took bridleways starting less than a quarter–mile from where I had stayed, leading westwards on to high ground.

From time to time I was asked questions about whether I was not afraid to walk by myself, about the risks of meeting 'funny men' as someone put it and I was forced to consider such questions seriously after my experience in Queen Elizabeth country park. I don't think that the idea of being molested had entered my head at all in the planning stage, and after my first indignant reaction to the incident I had more or less put it out of my mind; I certainly wouldn't put solo walking as a dangerous activity to be avoided at all costs. After all, being alive is a risky business, and too much caution would prevent anyone doing anything. Women should not be made to fear attack, rather encouraged to acquire confidence in their ability to deal with unpleasant situations.

My fears were of a different order: I had a healthy respect for large uncontrollable dogs, for example, and would brandish my crooked stick if growled or barked at. I didn't relish too much the thought of getting lost and was genuinely scared by the thought of being in mist and low cloud.

Walking solo even in relatively easy conditions necessarily entails responsibility for oneself alone. Making mistakes in navigation can sometimes simply mean extra miles to walk; in case of accident or injury it can be serious, and I was to become increasingly aware of this as I walked into lonelier country.

Anyway, today I was glad to be on my way again; the weather continued fair, the route straightforward; I met a few people walking their dogs, and, I noticed approvingly, keeping them well under control. Meeting a minor road at the top of the hill furnished with a convenient seat I stopped for a rest and saw a cuckoo fly by at close quarters, cuckooing vociferously. I watched it delightedly, the first cuckoo I had ever seen, surprising me by its size, as large as a jay. I remembered it was June 1st...in June I change my tune. Spring was over and I was walking into summer.

I descended into King's Somborne and walked on to cross the river Test, bordered by yellow flag-irises and king-cups and surprisingly full of water after a dry winter and spring, looking sparklingly clear, with trout lurking under the bridge. Swans sailed majestically by, and a dipper busied itself in mid-stream. I learned later that the whole of the Test valley has been designated a conservation area, hence the abundance of flowers and wildlife as well as clean rivers.

I found Corner Cottage in Houghton after going off for a mile in the wrong direction; as usual, I hadn't listened carefully enough to the directions. When found, it was an enchanting place, an old house set in the centre of a splendid garden with a swimming pool and spectacular views on all sides. My room was huge, converted to a self-contained flat from the playroom above the garage it had once been.

My friendly hostess ran me to the local John O' Gaunt pub, where I was greeted with 'the cook's in hospital so we're not serving food.' It seemed hard not even to be able to get some bread and cheese, but there it was. I walked back along a deserted road; it's wonderfully free on such occasions to be unburdened by a pack and hunger didn't prevent me enjoying the calm of the evening, the road crossing water meadows thronged with water–fowl and resplendent with wild–flowers of all kinds.

There was a picture window facing west from my room, and after dining on pitta and cheese I sat looking out over the countryside towards the setting sun. My eye rested first on the garden, a shaven lawn and freshly dug flower–beds, then on a brown field just turning green, a long hedge, a low line of hills. There wasn't a light to be seen, or a building and the only sound came from some tall trees where rooks were settling for the night. Beyond those hills, I knew, were other, further hills, and beyond them, more hills. As the sun sank and the sky changed colour from rose to apricot to lemon to turquoise it was almost possible to feel the world turning away from the sun. In the peaceful evening I feasted my eyes on the changing scene until the evening star appeared to signal the end of the performance. *June 2nd:* Sunday. Rendezvous time; at 9.20 Dick, who was to walk with me for the next two days, appeared in our well–travelled VW motor caravan. His first words were about my appearance: a) suntanned and b) thin. True, I'd lost a half stone in weight. My rucksack was loaded aboard to be taken to Salisbury and I set off on foot. I was again following the Romans along the straight line marked on my map leading to Old Sarum, the ancient city of Salisbury.

This Wiltshire Roman road was not given a name on the map but characteristic of its kind led me straight and true first on tarmac then bridleway. I went along lanes bordered with canter-bury bells and periwinkle, seeing pheasant, a hare, and a deer, to Middle Winterslow where the road did a series of un–Roman squiggles and there were unexpectedly steep hills. Beyond the village, where a party of about fifty ramblers were having an animated discussion about the route, the Roman road reasserted itself and led me into woods with a confusing number of paths. Dick coming in the opposite direction from Salisbury was having similar route–finding uncertainties so it was with some relief that we found our paths crossing as we reached the road to Pitton. We walked on and stopped in warm sunshine to lunch on home-made bread with home-grown lettuce, the kind of food which I had been sorely missing.

Back on the not altogether clear line of the Roman road we were lulled into a sense of false confidence in each other's route-finding abilities and thereupon proceeded to get well and truly lost, leaving the line of route for an obstacle course across fields and fences; an entertaining if protracted afternoon's walking. Back on course, we walked through the well-kept Clarendon estate, observing Salisbury cathedral spire coming nearer, to reach the car where Dick had parked it and drive to our B&B on the Bournemouth road. There was a good pub meal to compensate for spending a night in town, and a heavy shower, the first measurable rain in twelve days. Dick had brought me mail and a changes of clothes.

The Romans were not the only road-builders of ancient times in these parts, but were preceded by early hill-top settlers using drove roads to take them along the summit of the chalk downs and so avoiding the dangers of the inaccessible forested valleys; in planning my route I had looked on the maps for these ancient highroads as often providing scenic and practically direct cross-country routes. We were to follow drove roads for the next two days, bringing us to Warminster from where I would aim for Trowbridge and Bath.

June 3rd: We walked through the narrow streets of Salisbury to go through the cathedral close and past the cathedral, its famous spire clad in scaffolding like that of Winchester. We toiled up a steep hill to reach the ancient Salisbury Way. This follows the broad chalk ridge between the Nadder valley to the north and the Ebbe valley to the south, a prehistoric route which must have seemed particularly attractive to travellers, providing an open passage between two wet forested valleys. The track, still well preserved, must for centuries have been in almost constant use as the main road from Salisbury to the west. During the stage coach era it formed part of the route from London to Exeter until superseded in the nineteenth century by the A30 road built along the valley, and, of course, by the railroads.

The track, tarmac at first, soon became a green lane heading directly along the ridge, with views back to the cathedral spire still in sight long after we had left the city boundaries. We walked between fences to pass the stands of the racecourse. On the clear track and with our luggage divided between Dick and myself we made good progress in cool conditions with the wind now in the north.

The drove road goes on to join the A30 road near Shaftesbury, but we followed it only as far as the Iron Age hill settlement of Chislebury, one of the ancient earthworks with which this part of the country abounds. Chislebury has a spectacular position on a promontory of the ridge reaching out above the valley to the north. We followed its surrounding excavated ditch looking for but failing to find the right of way marked on the map which would take us down to the small village of Fovant. Frustrated by a ploughed field covered in gleaming white chalky stones, and guarded by an impenetrable barbed wire fence we retreated to continue along the track and to find a way down in another quarter–mile, through woods and along a shaven hillside, below the regimental badges carved into the chalk of the escarpment; the first of these I had learned was executed by Australian soldiers during World War 1.

Our path emerged on the main A30 road outside the Cross Keys Inn, where we had booked a room. The building dates back to the fifteenth century, but can have been much used as a travellers' halt only since the A30 was driven through the valley. Nowadays, with motorways siphoning off much of its traffic, the A30 bids fair to revert to a country road. The Cross Keys, however, does not lack atmosphere, with its oak beams and low ceilings.

Watching TV news we learned of Prince William's cracked skull and the royal dash to hospital

Leaving Fovant next morning we turned north, first by minor road to the village of Chilmark, rather confused by the fact that all the signposts we came to were pointing to RAF Chilmark, and nowhere else; RAF Chilmark wasn't even marked on our map. Rather fearful of trespassing on government property, we went unchallenged as we passed the various gates and guardrooms, speculating about what went on behind the high fences.

After Chilmark, with the terrain now agreeing with the map, we were back on to drove roads, more ancient earthworks, broad downland in pastel blues and greens, and wide views north in crystal clear air over the Wylye valley to Salisbury plain, with showerclouds sweeping over but missing us. At one point we met a huge flock of sheep herded ahead of shepherds on motorcycles; this reminded us of the drove roads of the Cevennes in France, where sheep are driven for the 'transhumance', the movement of flocks from the plains to the hills for summer grazing. In the Cevennes the sheep wear bells and are decorated with ribbons and rosettes in blue and red and the shepherds wear drab clothing which looks little different from that worn by shepherds of past centuries, but contrasting with this modernised way of herding sheep on Salisbury Downs.

The drove road finally deposited us on to quite undrove–like country roads, much more like those made by Chesterton's rolling English drunkard. We found a series of intricate field footpaths linking villages, pub to church, crossed a new by–pass and a river, and, most satisfactorily, climbed a hill and crossed a nature reserve to finish up in the centre of Warminster. The Farmer's Hotel, where we had booked, was for all the world like a French hotel, a tall gaunt building standing on a street corner, comfortable, unpretentious, and with a good dining–room. Tomorrow Dick and I were to part company, so there was sorting out and admin to do, and the realisation that soon I was going to be turning north after all the stepping westward. I had walked 162 miles in 14 days, which was well within my target distance, so was feeling optimistic about the next stages.

June 5th: The promised rain started as Dick and I parted at Warminster station, he to catch the train to Salisbury to recover the car and drive home, I to walk on to Trowbridge then Bath. This was the beginning of the long unsettled spell which was to continue throughout June. Looking at the map I decided to use minor roads as much as possible for this stage, my objective the Kennet and Avon canal at Trowbridge which I would then follow to Bath.

It rained relentlessly all day, cold penetrating rain, and I regretted that I had sent my Goretex cagoule back to base, leaving me with only a light rather inadequate waterproof. I put my head down and plodded on; every mile now was bringing me closer to the Cotswolds and a clear path north. The few villages I came to seemed devoid of friendly pubs so I crouched by a farm gate to eat lunch and hoped for better things at Trowbridge.

I followed a path by the river Biss to lead me into town, then found myself in a housing estate with no clear way through, a rather nightmarish section where my wet and dishevelled state made me self–conscious among townsfolk and schoolchildren. I hadn't booked ahead and found that somehow I had lost the tourist accommodation list which I had picked up at Warminster. Rather desperately I fought my way into town, arriving at the local tourist office just a few minutes before it was due to close. On the way I had narrowly escaped being run down by a post office van, and was beginning to realise that it was the towns rather than the country which presented hazards. After walking on traffic–free lanes and paths it takes a conscious effort to become accustomed to fast traffic.

At the tourist office they dealt patiently with my request for accommodation, not only telephoning around but ultimately taking me there by car, to a suburban house in a quiet road, where I was greeted with tea, comfort, and later a good meal. For the first time on this walk I had wet socks to take off and was grateful for a warm room.

June 6th: The Kennet and Avon canal, dating from the late eighteenth century before railways made obsolete the use of waterways to carry heavy freight, originates with the river Kennet near Reading where it flows into the Thames. The canal crosses Berkshire and Wiltshire to descend in a series of locks to the river Avon near Bath, thus making a continuous link between the Bristol Channel and the North Sea. After years of disuse and neglect the Kennet and Avon was rescued by an enthusiastic body of volunteers who as the Kennet and Avon Trust led the work of restoration, to make the canal navigable again. Evidence of its growing popularity can be seen in the numbers of brightly coloured narrowboats which used to house bargees and their families but now provide a peaceful means of spending a holiday away from roads.

I walked through central Trowbridge and asked a traffic warden for directions. Across busy roads and through an industrial estate, my exit was as unscenic as my entrance. On the whole I was rather glad to leave Trowbridge.

By the time it reaches Bradford–on–Avon the canal has passed its summit and is well on its way to join the River Avon, staying high and crossing a sequence of aqueducts to carry it across river and railway. Here the surroundings were truly scenic, with views down the wooded slopes of a country park. Motorboats and canal narrowboats were gently chugging along; more people appeared, walking their dogs or simply walking. A swan led a group of cygnets downstream, and banks of yellow flag–irises bordered the towpath.

At Avoncliffe I somehow managed to lose the canal towpath, in the confusion caused by canal, road, rail and river all converging and crossing, and found myself instead on a grassy riverside path. This came as a welcome variation to towpath walking, and I stopped to eat lunch in a meadow full of summer flowers. I found myself in Freshford, a picture book village with houses built in honey–coloured stone. The way back to the canal involved a climb giving me a taster of the steepness of West-country hills, something of a shock to the system after the level walking I had been doing. During this diversion I had crossed yet another county boundary, into Avon.

Regaining the towpath I crossed the Dundas viaduct, taking the canal high above the river and railway below, a magnificently engineered feature. I met a real long–distance walker coming in the opposite direction, moving so fast he hardly had time to respond to my greeting, then a friendly young woman on a bicycle who offered sweets and encouragement. At this point I was beginning to feel that I had had too long a day, and was conscious that I had some miles yet to go. I thought how strange that the pain doesn't seem to show!

Some time later I turned a corner and gasped at the beauty of the city of Bath, its architecturally well–ordered stone buildings rising in tiers against the opposite hillside. The canal banks became more tailored, with trees, grass, and seats for the weary.

34

Eventually I came to two bridges where the canal went underground beneath main roads, and at the second one was directed by a helpful passer-by into Pulteney Street and the centre of town.

I walked down the wide thoroughfare between rows of elegant houses, my fatigue vanishing in delight at this beautiful city which I was seeing for the first time. It was almost too good to be true, as if somebody had thought of an ideal city then proceeded to build it. Whichever way the eye turned it saw the setting as being just right for where it was. Among the crowds of sightseers my self-consciousness faded, to be replaced by a sense of wonder that here was another aspect of the walk that I hadn't really bargained for, finding unexpected beauty in places where I had seen myself merely as a transient.

Pulteney Street brought me out in front of the Abbey, then to thread my way through the city to the guest house, one of many along the Weston road where I had booked for the night. This had been a long and tiring day, but its ending had been adequate compensation for a long walk and tomorrow I would be really turning north, on to the Cotswold Way.

I breakfasted with an international group, an Australian couple from Melbourne and a young Canadian woman from Vancouver. There was real travellers' talk, of far places, old aeroplanes, surfing and sightseeing. It was here that someone first asked 'Where is Beachy Head?' the question seeming to put my travels in perspective against world travel, and making me feel for the first time that I had come a long way from my starting point. I listened eagerly to descriptions of the sights to be seen in Bath, it seeming almost sinful to leave without doing some sight-seeing of my own. I did however have a timetable to keep to, so left, vowing to return another day.

Chipping Campden
Broadway
Cheltenham — Puckham
Prestbury Crossroads
GLOUCESTER-SHIRE Birdlip
Dursley
Bristol Old Sodbury
AVON Cold Ashton
Bath

Bath to Chipping Campden.

4: Alternative Cotswold Ways

Friday June 7th: The Cotswold Way follows the edge of the escarpment of Cotswold limestone which runs north–east from Bath and rears above the surrounding landscape like the crest of a frozen wave. To the west is a stretch of countryside reaching to the River Severn which parallels the Cotswold Way for fifty miles of its length, and beyond rise the hills of South Wales, among them the Brecon Beacons and Black Mountains. To the east a plateau tilts towards the valley of the River Thames which has its origin at Seven Springs on the uplands near Charlton Kings Common. The Way is a regional route created in 1970 by Gloucestershire County Council, and follows existing rights of way for the best part of a hundred miles from Bath to Chipping Campden.

Some study of the three maps covering the Cotswold Way left me with the suspicion that it took a rather more meandering course to arrive at Chipping Campden than I thought was necessary for somebody bound for Birmingham. The lines of red diamonds which on the one–inch map indicate a long–distance footpath squiggled about rather alarmingly in their efforts to follow the line of cliffs faithfully. I was sure that there was good reason for this in the sights and views to be seen, but thought that I could do without some of them. I resolved that I would as far as possible keep on my northerly track, using the Cotswold Way only where it kept to the same course.

First I had to find the Cotswold Way, so I took a compass bearing north from Weston village, up a stony track, emerging on a hilltop by a farmhouse, and finding there a waymark bearing one of the tenpence–size white spots which the Cotswold Way has adopted as its own. Looking rather suspiciously at the weather, which was blowing up, I set off along a well–marked path heading reassuringly northwards.

After the built–up crossing through Warminster and Trowbridge and the crowded streets of Bath, lovely though the town was, it was good to be out in open country and to be on high ground again, looking at the showers all around but none of them coming my way. I came to Prospect Stile, at 238 metres, and stopped to look at the view, then jumped as a man came over the hill behind me. Queen Elizabeth Forest must have impressed me more than I thought.

It was all right, though. I thought at first he was the farmer, but he was just out walking his dog, and we talked about litter and rights of way and the weather. He went off and I said a last farewell to Bath.

Soon after this I missed a right turning and found myself among the manicured lawns and well–cared for houses of North Stoke, with an unwanted climb back on to the escarpment. Cotswold hills are steep, reminding me of the lanes climbing on to Dartmoor from the Devon river valleys. For the first time on the walk I was walking into the wind; although English weather typically comes from the west I been favoured with an east wind blowing me along most of the way from Eastbourne. Now it blew strong and cold from the north–west, bringing up clouds and spreading a grey murk, almost like mountain mist.

After the open slopes of the chalk downs, this was unfamiliar country to me, with stone farms hidden in steep–sided valleys; small streams bordered with celandine threaded their way through these dells. I lost the route crossing one valley and had to make my way through a lumpy wet field to find my way back to the path under the eye of a farmer. I was now on the second half of the dogleg which the Cotswold Way takes from Bath, first north–west to North Stoke, then a longer leg north–east to cross the main A46 road near Cold Ashton.

I did more ups and downs, and on the final climb to meet the main road met a tramp, looking just as tramps are supposed to look, with numerous layers of clothing, much facial hair, and carrying an assortment of plastic carriers. It was quite impossible to guess what his age might be. He asked me the way to Bath and I tried to direct him, thinking that without a map it might not be too easy to follow the Cotswold Way. I wondered, but didn't like to ask, what he would do in Bath once arrived there.

The murk was really descending now with thunder rumbling in the distance, and I hastened along the lane to Cold Ashton, finding that a change in pace didn't seem to trouble my stiff ankle too much. Cold Ashton really did feel cold, set high on the Cotswold plateau but how nice to be in a tiny village after the towns of the last three days. I walked through the village, to find my farm B&B, where I had to take off my boots downstairs, muddy for the first time in seventeen days.

In the evening I walked through the well-kept village, past the church and across two fields to the White Hart, where I dined cheaply and well; as I returned the mist had cleared to a red sunset, and I looked down the southern hillside into the beautiful St Catherine's valley with enfolding green hills dotted with Cotswold sheep, and with stone walls reminding me of the Derbyshire uplands.

June 8th: I breakfasted with a couple from Chester, on a stop-over on their way to the Westcountry, discovering we had mutual acquaintances. Situated just a few miles away from where the M4 motorway cuts a slash across the area at Tormarton, this must be a peaceful resting place for travellers; perhaps it always was, before the age of the motorway.

Sheep were being brought in for the shearing as I left, the sound of their bleating following long after I was out of sight, on another misty grey morning, rather like Wales or Scotland. I wrote in my log 'too strenuous really, my foot hurting on uneven ground, countryside changing, fields full of cereal crops, kestrels, swallows, chaffinches, skylarks, and a cuckoo back.'

I descended into a wood, across a narrow plank bridge, and into open country up a steep hill to reach Dyrham village. I exchanged greetings with people on horseback, who I observed were privileged to ride through Dyrham Park, while walkers were channelled on to the hillside outside its walls; it was a fine walk nevertheless on a green rising track with views across a valley to Hinton Hill with its summit hill fort. Anti-climax followed, a trudge across cereal fields with the traffic roar of the M4 motorway coming closer. I arrived in the carpark adjoining the motorway simultaneously with the rain, and huddled at a picnic table to put on my inadequate waterproofs.

The crossing of the M4 entailed a hazardous roundabout offering no concessions to walkers, and I thankfully escaped from traffic noise into quiet lanes for a wet afternoon's walk to Old Sodbury and my B&B in the Old Vicarage at the top of the hill a few yards from the Cotswold Way. I shared the dining–room with a large family party, ten of them, on their way to a christening in Bristol, rather like a French family I thought, three generations with well–behaved small children. Dinner was home–made steak and kidney pie, trifle and cheese, in generous portions.

Back in my room I found that I had now walked two hundred miles, but started to worry about my slow progress, with the aim to be in Chipping Campden in a week's time. I would need to increase the distances to be covered in the next few days, and decided that my plan to devise an alternative Cotswold Way would have to be put into operation.

June 9th: Sunday. There were groups of day walkers about as I crossed a hillside and descended a lane to Little Sodbury, then across fields passing a beautiful tree–shaded lake under the folds of the hills. I went on to Horton, a well–tailored village where the Cotswold Way takes a wide sweep to the east, climbing the hillside invitingly. This was definitely not on my line of march, and I took to my own route, due north along a little road which wound its way along the hillside at a lower level, to emerge opposite the church at Hawkesbury. The next section turned into a farm track, a deserted unfenced lane with grass growing down its middle; I began to enjoy my alternative Cotswold Way, and gloated over the miles I was saving by taking this route.

The skies darkened as I approached Hillesley and the threatened rain began in earnest as I came into the village, bidding fair to turn into a cloudburst. I made a dash for the pub which by good fortune was a few steps away; it was full of Sunday eaters, drinkers, and smokers. Somehow I wormed my way to the bar and found sanctuary on a stool in a corner, where I was served in friendly fashion with sandwiches and coffee, a second helping brought without my asking for it. By the time I had finished the rain had eased to a trickle, and I emerged to find a stream running down the road which was covered in debris; in one dip there was a small flood.

A mile north of Hillesley I crossed the border into Gloucester, beginning now to lose count of counties, and earlier than expected I was approaching Wotton–under–Edge so decided to walk on to Dursley, another six miles distant by my alternative route. I briefly renewed acquaintance with the Cotswold Way, then struck steeply up Coombe Lane with views back over countryside I had crossed, still under a stormy–looking sky. At the summit I was confronted with more cars and people than I had seen all day; a car rally was in progress, its finish in a nearby field.

Miraculously the squalls which seemed to be everywhere were avoiding just where I was, as I walked along deserted lanes leading down an enchanting valley with wooded hills folding into it. I climbed a breathtakingly steep hill, where a peacock crossed my path, to arrive at a spot where the world was spread at my feet: plain, motorway, and the Bristol Channel, and far away the misty Welsh hills with rainclouds lapping their summits. Now there was a real sense of distance having been covered. I had walked from one sea to within sight of another. The day's walk had been immensely worthwhile and I was well on schedule once again.

I descended into Dursley and walked through the traffic–free precinct to find my night's B&B in a large homely house. Mrs Williams clearly liked looking after people, and served a splendid evening meal to myself and two young Swedish women walking the Cotswold Way. We ate soup, venison in cider, and a wonderful pear and mince pie with cream; good conversation added to the enjoyment. I wrote in my diary:

> My room has a view over the next section of the Cotswold Way, to Coaley Peak; looks enticing, but what weather! Like Wales, mist closing in, a blustery south–west wind blowing, rain, lilacs shedding their petals on the lawn like confetti, temperature no more than 12 or so. Flaming June!

June 10th: I left Dursley thinking it a nice cheerful small town, and wondering if with its major engineering works it had escaped the worst of the recession. My second day's attempt at an alternative Cotswold Way was less successful; there were a number of likely−looking lines of red dots on my map going in the right direction, turning out to be non−existent on the ground or badly overgrown with nettles and brambles. After two abortive attempts to create my own route I headed back for the Cotswold Way proper, deciding that I would have done better to have kept to the way−markings in the first place.

Thoroughly wetted by what was to be the only heavy shower of the day I emerged on to the escarpment near Coaley Peak to be greeted by a brisk wind sweeping in from the Atlantic, the kind that my mother used to call idle, and another spectacular view; the Cotswold Way lived up to its reputation as being like a cliff footpath in taking me along the edge of the steep escarpment with the countryside below flowing away in waves of brown and green to the wide river Severn where it became the Bristol Channel and beyond it to the Forest of Dean. Near the viewpoint at Frocester hill there were children flying kites, and a kestrel was hovering.

I left the escarpment to cross clover fields, peeping into Nympsfield Long Barrow as I went, into beech woods where the track bordered the minor road and like most accessible sections of long−distance paths was well provided with waymarks. (It tends to be in places where the route is least obvious that waymarks disappear.) As I was emerging into a clearing a dog fox walked unhurriedly across my path less than six feet away seeming totally to ignore my presence.

I found an alternative route down a steep slope supplied in places with rudimentary steps, then crossed fields and lanes to King's Stanley. There was a roadwalk from here to cross river Frome, canal, railway and main A419 road, this yet another landmark, taking me north of the Bristol Channel. I was just about at sea−level, with steep fields to climb to regain lost height. This was laborious and I began to realise that after nine days' continuous walking from Winchester I was in need of a rest day. I looked forward to arriving in Prestbury in two days' time, where I was to spend two nights with friends.

At the top of the hill I found a telephone box to phone ahead for the night's lodging at Randwick, which turned out to be only ten minutes' walk further up the road, a converted seventeenth century farmhouse owned by the local primary school teacher, who gave me another good evening meal. There was a expansive view from my bedroom window, looking over the Frome valley to the hills I had just crossed; fluffy pink clouds dappled the evening sky. I watched TV news, to learn that England had defeated the West Indies in the Headingly Test, the first time for twenty–two years; it was the seventieth birthday of the Duke of Edinburgh.

One of my two breakfast companions called me 'me duck', and I discovered he came from Coventry. Things were changing again, I was leaving the West country and would soon be in the heart of England.

June 11th: As I left the house the rain started again, not particularly enthusiastically. 'Scarcely one–cagoule weather' I wrote in my diary. Rejoining the Cotswold Way at Bird–in–Hand, I somehow missed a vital turning. I followed a path which led me along a spur down a grassy hillside between woods giving a view forward to a stone farmhouse in a green valley, and more green hills beyond. I was charmed by this landscape, thinking it like a child's picture of the countryside, so much so that I failed to check my direction, and found myself about two miles off route at a junction of main roads. A woman farmer stopped her car to ask which way I was going, disappointed that I wouldn't be using the right of way across her field! On the contrary, I had to follow the main road into Painswick, saved by the sidewalk which the local authority had considerately provided.

Once I had escaped the lethal traffic on the A46, Painswick was quiet. I trawled its back streets, finding a coffee house between the almshouses and the church, then bought cheese roll, banana and chocolate from the well–stocked Spa supermarket. The friendly woman at the checkout told me that her son was at this time doing the West Highland Way.

The rain had stopped by now, so I went on out of town, leaving the suburban streets to cross the golfcourse on green tracks, soft underfoot. The May blossom was just about over and wild roses were coming into bloom, with honeysuckle climbing over every wall. Somewhere near here there is a place called Paradise! As I crossed a road a car stopped and its driver told me that he'd done the Cotswold Way last year and hoped I'd enjoy it as much as he had; he finished by saying 'God bless you', which made me feel good, unbeliever though I am it's nice to know that people wish you well.

I went on into beechwoods and a nature reserve, to Cranham Corner and another alternative Cotswold Way. This proved to be a mistake; the unclassified road, looking a harmless minor by-way on my map, had been 'improved', and after a while I forsook it to descend into woods below the road and find the path where it came in from Cooper's Hill. The path kept high along the hillside, with views through beech trees over the Forest of Dean; more bad weather was sweeping in from the west. I arrived on the road at the top of Birdlip Hill just a few yards from Beechmount where I was to spend the night. Today had been a short one, the last of my third week, and I was within easy striking distance of Cheltenham and the prospect of a rest day.

There were six pairs of boots in the vestibule of the guesthouse when I came indoors after doing some telephoning. I talked with the owner of one pair, a north-to-souther doing seventeen-miles-a-day stages. He said he had had the same week's holiday every year, and this was the worst weather yet. I couldn't help being on the whole relieved that we weren't having heatwave conditions, feeling the cool days more comfortable for walking, but thought it would be nice to have some sun. We sat in the lounge watching the tree-tops tossing in the wind and with the rain beating on the windows, looking less like June than October.

Walking the Cotswold Way from the north involves less climbing, always a consideration in linear routes, the river Avon at Bath being almost at sea level against Chipping Campden at a height of about 150 metres. Not a great deal, but walkers do notice this kind of thing. Against the advantage gained by going downhill to Bath, if going south you are likely to walk into bad weather, as was happening this summer.

June 12th: The rain had stopped, and it was an exhilarating

44

walk to the viewpoint at Barrow Wake, with its panoramic view over the vale of Gloucester. I did another short cut and walked for a horrendous mile along the A436 road, thankfully to recover the Cotswold Way leading to the escarpment and woods through fields full of vetch, campion and clover. Little furry animals scuttled away into the undergrowth and the view opened out to valley, reservoir and Cheltenham.

Almost as easily as I'd found the Cotswold Way I lost it again in a wood with too many unmarked paths, and descended the steep hillside to find myself trapped in a field apparently leading only into someone's garden. Feeling demoralised I extricated myself by using the house driveway, finding afterwards that I needn't have worried about trespassing; the track leading down to the road was marked as a right of way on my map. I arrived on the A40 road just as the rain started and made tracks for the Reservoir Inn a hundred yards away. I scuttled to its rear carpark and up an outside staircase to the bar.

I had coffee and sandwiches, then left as the rain stopped, to cross the road and follow the track over the dam of the Dowdeswell reservoir, to find the path climbing steeply to Dow-deswell Wood, following a marching line of pylons. A fierce wind was blowing across the fields and, too early for my rendezvous, I took shelter behind a hedge to catch up on my log, then walked down the road to Puckham crossroads in the teeth of the wind, realising that the Cotswolds, with a height here of almost three hundred metres, have the characteristics of higher hills. I arrived at the crossroads to find Phil Powell in the act of driving up from Prestbury to ferry me to his house for a welcome break.

I am continually amazed by how often this kind of arrangement works out successfully, when a meeting arranged simply by studying a map comes about at the time and in the place planned for.

It was lovely to be with old friends, and next day was a good one not to be walking the Cotswold Way, cold and wet, with the wind battering the windows. I got myself up to date with mail, and did washing and vital chores, even ironing shirt and trousers so that I looked 'less like a bag lady' said Phil. I packed a large parcel for home, exchanging inadequate waterproofs for my Goretex cagoule. I checked up on progress, finding that having walked two hundred and sixty miles in twenty-two days I was well within my target average of ten miles per day, but was alarmed to discover that I had a twenty-one mile stage next day to Broadway; I looked for another alternative Cotswold Way.

On still another grey cool morning Phil took me back to Puckham crossroads, where I followed the Cotswold Way along the escarpment, to leave it again where at a TV mast it strikes north for Cleeve Hill. I chose instead to cut across the common to retrieve the path on its return journey, thus cutting off three miles from the day. This was a pleasant high-level walk, and I descended to Winchcombe along flower-fringed country lanes, just in time for coffee.

I left the Cotswold Way for a riverside path followed by an unremitting trudge along more lanes. A small dog ran out of a cottage gate and snapped at my heels. 'He doesn't like the noise of your stick,' said the woman who came to call him in! After the show villages of Stanton and Stanway the country began to open out to give views first over the Vale of Gloucester, then the Vale of Evesham, the steep-sided valleys disappearing, to be replaced by park-like fields dotted with oak trees and with horses grazing. There was a sense of generous acres of country-side ahead waiting to be explored. More county boundaries were to be crossed, today from Gloucester to Worcestershire, and tomorrow I would be in Warwickshire and starting yet another long-distance footpath.

Broadway has been so much photographed that the village inspires a sense of *déjà vu*. I came in from the field and river path to find crowds of people and a main road cutting what must once have been a quiet community in half. I have no liking for tourist honeypots, so hastened to find my B&B. Broadway offers less than could be hoped for in eating places, at least after six-thirty, and the Hare and Hounds served indifferent fish and chips with inedible vegetables, Broadway not appearing to have even an honest to goodness fish and chip shop. I retired to hear an adverse weather forecast.

June 15th: Dame Peggy Ashcroft is dead, I heard on the

morning news, the end of another era. Approaching Shakespeare country as I was, I thought of her marvellous rendering of Portia, perhaps making a connection with the weather; certainly there was plenty of gentle rain dropping from heaven. Broadway was engulfed in misty clouds.

I climbed out of town through dripping fields to reach the Broadway tower. It is said that it is possible to see thirteen counties from its summit, today it was difficult even to see the Tower! I followed a woman walking her dog to the country park entrance, where a few motorists were sitting glumly in their cars, then continued through soaking wet crops to reach the road at Mile Drive. I sat upon a thoughtfully provided roadside seat and decided that I was at risk of hypothermia, so dug out spare clothes and gloves and wrapped myself up, the first time on the walk I had needed all my Arctic gear.

Chipping Camden was full of Saturday shoppers with unbrellas. I wandered up and down its High Street, noting with satisfaction that the central lamp standard in the square bore a new waymark, the logo of the Heart of England Way, depicting a group of tall trees. I went into the wine bar for soup and sandwiches, realising that I was still shivering, then crossed the road to the Bantam tea–shop, where I was to keep yet another unlikely rendezvous. I was on my second cup of coffee when in walked Lesley Dunn, who had travelled from London that morning by train to Moreton–in–Marsh, then by bus to keep our appointment. It was extraordinarily good to see her at this distance from home. Lesley was to walk with me for the next three days, and I knew would be a cheerful and resourceful companion. Delighted that our plan had worked out, we spent an hour exchanging news, then set off into the still steadily falling rain.

Uttoxeter

Derby

Abbots Bromley

Lichfield

Kingsbury

Meriden

Birmingham

Coventry

Henley in Arden

Worcester

Alcester

Stratford on Avon

Mickleton

Chipping Campden

Chipping Campden to Uttoxeter

5: England's Heart

O Pastoral heart of England! like a psalm
Of green days telling with a quiet beat –
O wave into the sunset flowing calm
O tired lark descending on the wheat!
Lies it all peace beyond that western fold
Where now the lingering shepherd sees his star
rise upon Malvern? Paints an age of gold
Yon cloud with prophecies of linked ease –
Lulling this land, with hills drawn up like knees
To drowse beside her implements of war?

Arthur Quiller-Couch

The Heart of England Way was for me an indispensable link
between the Westcountry and the northern Peak District and
moorlands. The way is an eighty-mile route leading from
Chipping Campden in the south to Cannock Chase in the north.
Groups of enthusiastic local walkers knitted together the series of
rights of way which make up the path, and the efforts of the
Heart of England Way Steering Committee have recently resulted
in the path's adoption by the County Councils whose territory it
crosses. Waymarking of the route is now complete, with green
and white logos sprouting at every turning.

People who drive through the middle of England will usually
see only the views from the motorways which converge on the
Midland conurbations. Spaghetti Junction may be considered
more characteristic of the heart of England than is the Forest of
Arden. In its course, however, and astonishingly, the Heart of
England Way manages to thread its way between the major cities
of Birmingham and Coventry, acknowledging only in passing the
built-up and industrialised heartland. Instead there is varied,
often beautiful, and little-known country to be explored.

I had taken care to provide myself with a guide to the Heart of England Way. It was a good guide, presenting just one problem: the guide was designed for those walking the route from north on Cannock Chase to south at Chipping Campden. Reading a guide backwards must be something like reading Chinese; there is a constant struggle to remember that right coming south means left going north, and the need to do this was to add some interesting complications to the walk in the next few days.

It may have been because of our being novices at reading route instructions backwards that Lesley and I spent the hour after leaving the Bantam teashop wandering in the mist trying to find the Heart of England Way. We set forth from the signpost in the main square, then totally failed to find another waymark until, prowling around the outskirts of a rather unpromising school building, Lesley spotted one through a hedge leading into a very wet field full of cabbages. We squelched our way through this and other equally soggy fields, the chief interest being in the variety of crop: corn, oats, and cabbages. The rain fell relent-lessly, and we peered about in the mist looking for waymarks which now appeared sufficiently often to reassure us that we were on course. Fields led to a country lane, and then, as we descended a green hillside, the clouds parted to reveal village and church of Middleton below, our destination for the night. Beyond the village we saw Meon Hill, last outpost of the Cotswold ridge.

On reaching our B&B we felt fairly disorganised after a thorough wetting, I thankful for Goretex but finding that my Brasher boots didn't keep out water. We dried out and went to the pub across the road for supper, with clouds clearing to give a stormy-lookng sunset.

June 16th: Sunday. We breakfasted with an American couple, nutritionists whose job was assessing the virtues of brands of breakfast cereal, thus with an interest in the assortment provided at the B&B. I asked how they, as experts, rated the numbers of cereals on the market. Was told that they are all reasonably nutritious, but grossly overpriced; 'You would do just as well with a slice of wholemeal bread and a vitamin pill.' Well, yes, but I think I do like some variety in my diet.

I was finding overnight stops to be of continual variety and interest. Being invited into somebody's home for bed and breakfast strikes me as being rather like the practice of taking a TV camera into a home in that for a brief period you are able to have a fly-on-the wall view of how other people live. I never fail to be touched and charmed by the fact that people are prepared to open their homes in this way to whoever happens to turn up on the doorstep. There's a subtle difference between staying at a B&B and at a hotel in that the hotel offers an impersonal service, where, however caring that service may be, your activities are your affair and you are not expected to reveal what they may be, whereas most people who offer B&B do so because they are interested in people and want to know about you.

There's also the interest of the people who share the accommodation for the night. I was becoming skilled in assessing how people might respond if I disclosed that I was walking end-to-end. There were those who showed enthusiastic and knowledgeable interest, or genuinely wanted to know what it was like, against some who had no concept of how or why people wanted to go long-distance walking when there were other perfectly feasible means of getting about the countryside involving less trouble and expense. I grew to recognise such people by the blank expressions and speedy change of topic when I said what I was doing.

Up to now I had been treated like a family treasure by Felicity; had stayed in a converted hop kiln with a retired naval captain and wife; in country pubs and in a town guesthouse, where, to my disgust, I was asked to pay for the pot of tea on arrival, the only time this happened in the whole walk. The cost of B&B seemed to bear little relation to the facilities offered; in the place which I remember with most pleasure I was charged only £10 for the night's lodging.

There is, of course, one irreducible constant: the juice, cereal, egg, bacon, sausage and tomato, tea and toast served for breakfast. Because I often lack appetite for a large meal early in the day I soon got into the habit of taking uneaten food with me; the second breakfasts that I was able to have became an enjoyable tradition of the walk, something to look forward to in mid–morning when spirits were flagging.

We left Middleton in a rainstorm, walking past village gardens full of geraniums and delphiniums to turn into a sad lane bordered with disused glasshouses, roofs sagging and panes of glass missing, casualties of the recession. We climbed into wet fields, and were at once assailed by stern notices admonishing us to keep to the path. It would have been difficult to do otherwise; we were surrounded by waist–high cereal crops which had a remarkable ability to hold water. Each step released a small shower–bath on to trousers and boots, so that we felt rained on from the heavens above and the earth beneath. We also had our first encounters with heart of England stiles, a succession of fiendishly devised obstacles to progress.

Descending to the lane leading to Lower Quinton we somehow lost the Heart of England Way, and were roundly scolded by the farmer, who happened to drive up just as we were exiting, harmlessly we thought, by a convenient gate. Lesley was most indignant at the parting shot 'mind you shut the gate'. We began to feel unwanted.

Hurrying on under threatening skies we reached a road at Long Marston with convenient pub and timing just as the rain started. The pub was full of Sunday drinkers. 'I like your crooked stick,' said one.

The afternoon tested our navigation skills; we spent a frustrat–ing half–hour exploring an outsize field trying to find the way out, climbed some more mega–stiles, and came into Dorsington, where there was a father's day fete, complete with Morris dancers. We stayed to watch and photograph this very English display, assuring us that we really were in the Heart of England.

We followed the river to Bidford–on–Avon, then to our delight found a Roman road, a section of Rykneld Street, to follow along a scintillating avenue of laburnums, up and over the hillside. There was a rainbow leading us on, and a blue and white striped hot air balloon hung over the hills ahead. We crossed a bypass and descended into Alcester, its name deriving from Roman occupation but having closer associations with the Forest of Arden. We realised that we had walked into Shakespeare country.

The Swan Hotel where we had booked had seen better days, but our room was large and comfortable, and there was a huge pink bath. The Swan didn't serve meals, so we dashed across the road to the Cross Keys to find much needed food before they stopped serving, chicken chasseur and lemon cheesecake.

June 17th In town next morning, we walked past old timbered houses, restored, no doubt, but looking much as they must have looked in Shakespeare's day, and climbed up the hill out of town towards the remnants of the Forest of Arden, relieved to find fewer stiles than yesterday. It was a better morning, and the sun was drying out the fields.

The countryside improved, with rounded green tree–topped hills, a sufficiency of waymarks, and wide views, the feeling of being on a ridge. We passed close to the village of Bearley, where I had once spent a week helping to harvest potatoes in the post–war days, went through a wood, and came down to a road with a green hill opposite, aptly if unimaginatively named Round Hill. We crossed one field which kept below the crest of the hill, and went through a gate into the next; here Lesley stopped in her tracks, saying 'Do you see that animal over there?'

I looked, and saw, unmistakably, a large bull drinking from a cattle trough which lay directly on our route beside the next gate. Now, in general, I regard farm animals as basically harmless; they go about their business and I go about mine. But I do treat bulls with due respect. There is something about the solid bulk of these animals which convinces me that in any close encounter I would come off worst; so I tend to give any bull a wide berth. We retired behind a hedge to consider our next move.

We soon discovered that there was no way round the bull, all other exits from our field being well secured. Looking at the map we found that to do an alternative route would add several miles to the day's march. Following the dictum 'when in doubt, eat', which I learned many years ago from a cyclist friend, we found a sunny spot, and rather glumly ate our sandwiches. After this I took a cautious look through the gate; wherever the bull was it had removed itself from our path, so carefully hugging the side of the field with an eye to escape over a barbed–wire fence into the neighbouring wood, we crept along, observing that the animal in question had now retired up the hill to a shady spot under some trees and appeared to be taking a siesta. The crisis over, we continued on our way, relieved when we had safely shut the next gate with the bull on its far side.

There followed a delightful afternoon's walk across Wawensmoor; a field full of grazing Hereford cows, with rabbits scuttling under our feet, led into old woods and out onto smooth grassy slopes, looking over a wide valley to the east, a long vista with what seemed like the whole of the Midland plain before us. Descending into the flatlands we again lost the waymarks and found ourselves confronted by another angry farmer. 'Is it possible for you to be so stupid as to miss the waymarks?' he said.

There's little to be said in defence against such an accusation. Our attempts to be friendly and conciliatory were obviously going to cut no ice, and we slunk away with our tails between our legs, wondering what threat two eminently respectable middle–aged ladies could present in this well–ordered landscape.

We had to hug the verges for a half–mile walk along the busy main road into Henley–on–Arden, where we were dismayed to find no room at the inn or anywhere else along the High Street, the first time that this had happened to me on the walk so far. I had found previously that in most small towns or villages people if already full up would know of someone else who might not openly advertise accommodation, but would readily take in someone else's overflow, a bit like the wartime escape lines for aircrew. No such system seemed to be in operation in Henley–on–Arden, and the best we could learn was that there was a motel 'about a mile up the road' towards Birmingham.

It was a case of any port in a storm, so we set off rather disconsolately along the main road, dodging the rush–hour traffic, only half believing in the motel's existence and wondering if we really were going to have to walk all the way to Birmingham. It seemed a long mile, as such quests do, but just as we were contemplating turning back we turned a corner and found that we were there outside the motel. Our not having a car didn't seem to worry the business–like receptionist, and we soon found ourselves settling in, my first acquaintance with the motel way of life. I imagine this one was typical of its kind; a small cabin-like room with twin beds, a shower, tea-making facilities, and no room to swing a cat. I made a point of using the telephone to book accommodation ahead for the next two nights; once bitten....I discovered that during the day I had reached yet another century, to bring my total walked to three hundred miles.

June 18th: We had to make do with a rather inadequate continental breakfast then set off along the lane opposite, having decided to abandon the Heart of England Way on what was going to be a long day, using instead a succession of country lanes and small roads which went parallel to the route. The roads were pleasantly traffic-free, and bordered with the wild flowers which had been absent in the days of walking through intensively cultivated fields. We came to and crossed the Stratford-on-Avon Canal, climbed a hill between houses with gardens full of summer flowers, crossed the new bridge over the M40 Motorway, and found at Turner's Green the Navigation Inn just over the bridge of the Grand Union Canal, where we sat out over lunch another of the heavy rainstorms which seemed to be a feature of this part of the country, or perhaps merely a feature of a very wet month.

We walked on to the main road at Balsall Common, where Lesley was to leave me to catch a train south. Our parting words were drowned in the noise of thundering traffic and we went in opposite directions. I thought that I would miss Lesley's cheerful company and stoicism.

Next stop for me was Meriden, three or so miles further on. I picked up the Heart of England Way at Berkswell, following it through parkland to emerge in Birmingham suburbia. I was at my nearest point to Birmingham, just a handful of miles away, to the west and with Coventry equally close to the east. What was remarkable was the rural nature of the landscape. The region is criss-crossed with main roads and motorways, but between them lie many miles of quiet countryside.

Meriden has retained its character, the main A45 road bypassing it; in my researches I had been surprised at the apparent wealth of accommodation locally, finding out on the spot that the town benefits from being close to the National Exhibition Centre. Leaving the Heart of England Way I climbed a steep hill to find my B&B in a modern house at its summit. The man waiting at the gate greeted me warmly and said that he had earlier passed me in his car; he had considered offering me a lift and had decided against it thinking his offer would be misinterpreted.

I had at one time been an experienced hitch–hiker; in war–time and early post–war days this had been the most effective means of getting around, and I had travelled the length and breadth of the United Kingdom without any fears for my safety, although not without adventures. This was in the days before motorways, and long–distance drivers were often glad of company on long and slow journeys. Perhaps there has always been some risk about hitch–hiking which used to receive less media attention, but I find it rather sad that people nowadays can not be quite so carefree and equally sad that car–drivers cannot offer help without risking being misunderstood.

I wrote in my diary 'last day of week 4 and still no sign of summer, in two days it will be the solstice'. I ate the remains of my lunchtime food, listened to the news, and did some more forward planning. By Lichfield I would be in Staffordshire and leaving the Heart of England Way to aim for the Peak District. *June 19th*: I left, and walked into Meriden, to find to my delight that I had actually reached the heart of England! On the green sward outside a row of shops was a stone monument with an inscription which said that:

> *This ancient wayside cross has stood in the village*
> *for some 500 years and by tradition marks the*
> *CENTRE OF ENGLAND*
> *The cross was rebuilt on this site when the green was*
> *improved in celebration of the Festival of Britain*
> *AD 1951*

Coming so unexpectedly on this ancient cross in this insignificant small town so close to the industrial heartland had the effect of lifting my spirits immeasurably. Because I had set Birmingham in my sights as an intermediate objective on my journey through Britain, I could look ahead from this point to the Scottish border, and, psychologically speaking, go downhill for a while. I looked round for someone to whom I could say, 'I've come to Birmingham by way of Beachy Head and I've reached the Heart of England'. On this grey morning, with the rain just starting, no one seemed really interested; there were just a few people, mostly women, hurrying about their business, and probably not noticing the cross at all, the way one doesn't see things that have been around a long time. I had to hug my elation to myself.

I was to discover later that other places than Meriden lay claim to being the centre of England. The centre of Roman England is said to be at High Cross on the A5 where the Fosse Way crosses Watling Street. I tell myself, however, that boundaries in today's Britain have changed from Roman times, when Hadrian built his wall some miles outside what is now the Scottish border to keep out the barbarians. I'm quite happy to settle for Meriden.

On this unpromising morning I had again decided to forsake the Heart of England Way which was doing a fair number of squiggles to get to Kingsbury, my next objective, so set off along more unfrequented lanes, with the rain now falling determinedly. I was to find throughout that unclassified roads, the ones marked in little yellow lines on the Ordnance Survey map, had a fair chance of being little used, with heavy traffic nowadays keeping to trunk roads and motorways. The noise of the first of these, the A45, soon assailed my ears, and I was glad to leave it behind, and, in turn, the M6. Landmarks came in sight which hitherto I had seen only from inside a car, the first of these the Coleshill cooling towers. Coming to and passing these increased my sense of distance covered.

I rejoined the Heart of England way near Marston, where I came upon Kingsbury Water Park, a succession of flooded gravel-pits set in low woodland and heathland. So close to the populated Midlands, this must be a honeypot for weekend leisure, but on this Wednesday afternoon there were few people about; one sailing boat and a few fishermen, and plenty of waterfowl. After ten miles of road-walking it was a pleasure to walk along deserted tracks, then by the riverside, to cross a footbridge and climb the hill past the church into Kingsbury village.

I felt saddened by Kingsbury; here built around an old church was an attractive small community which had been cut in two by a main road along which traffic hurtled to reach the M42 motorway half a mile to the north. Just one pedestrian crossing linked the two halves of the village. And yet it seemed a friendly place; I went into the small general store in the single row of shops for supplies and was asked by the Asian woman at the check-out how far I had walked that day, and was advised not to buy the rolls because they were too stale.

The retired couple with whom I stayed in a tiny bungalow just across the road were equally friendly, interested in walking and bird-watching, and with a daughter studying music in London. After settling in I went to look for food. In such a small place I was surprised to find three pubs and a country club, and after some hesitation settled for the latter, a large new building with a huge carpark. Inside seemed at first deserted, but I found my way into the bar, furnished in what I would call fifties rococo; plastic-covered seating and formica tables and a bar with a surfeit of glass and bright metal. The large room had only three occupants, middle-aged men in working clothes although it was soon apparent from their talk that at least one of them was unemployed. A large television screen was showing a soap opera, I think East Enders. The place seemed forlorn, needing people and conversation to bring it to life.

I chose the vegetarian dish, cheap apple and mushroom stroganoff with rice, which was good and plentiful. I noted in my diary 'appetite returning, today I've eaten breakfast, two bananas, a roll and other goodies, but notice my trousers becoming looser. My ankle appreciated the road walking.' I came back to look at maps again and hear a better weather forecast, for warmer, sunnier weather.

June 20th: I had porridge for breakfast, eaten in friendly fashion in the kitchen, then left to cross the water park again, between banks of wild flowers. I noticed for the first time that there were poppies in bloom. I worked my way west and north around the northern perimeter of Birmingham, more horse-and-golf-course country, and crossed into Staffordshire near the huge traffic complex at Basset's Pole where three main trunk roads meet. More memories here of wartime days, when I was stationed as a transport driver at the RAF maintenance unit at Sutton Coldfield, and our nearest pub was the Basset's Pole. In those days the roads were virtually traffic–free and in recollection a world away from this maelstrom of roaring juggernauts.

I threw a salute to the Sutton Coldfield TV tower, another well–known landmark, and later in the day came to the A5 at Wall. Wall is at the halfway point on the journey from London to North Wales, along the remains of old Watling Street. I had chosen this crossing because of its associations with many family trips over the years.

Wall, Letoceum, has Roman Baths owned by the National Trust, but the mile of Roman road now a busy dual carriageway was fixed by Alfred the Great, whose statue I had last seen in Winchester, as the northern boundary of his Saxon kingdom with that of the Danelaw. The little road to Lichfield, reluctant to set itself against thunderous traffic, wriggles underneath the A5 before setting its course up the hill to Lichfield. The three spires of Lichfield Cathedral soon came into view, but before reaching my night's lodging in Gaia Lane behind it I had to run the gauntlet of the evening rush hour which infested the streets of the town, and was thankful to escape up the quiet side road.

The spires of the cathedral, visible for many miles around, are known as the Ladies of the Vale, the vale being that of the river Trent which, rising in Staffordshire, here turns north–east to mark the Derbyshire boundary. Here was more evidence that I was approaching the limestone hills and dales of the Peak District, but before starting on this eagerly anticipated section of the walk I was going to break off my journey for a three–day halt in Derby. I was beginning to feel the need of an extended rest after more than four weeks on the trail.

My B&B was in a lovely old house with a cathedral view, and the creature comforts which I was learning to value, hot bath, lots of tea, and TV; in the evenings there seemed little time for more than planning the next day's walk, watching the news, and sinking into bed once the business of finding somewhere to eat had been dealt with. This evening I walked through the now quiet streets of the town, occupied only by groups of young people who seemed to have nowhere else to go. I looked at the few open eating places, didn't fancy any of them, and finished by buying fish and chips which I took into the memorial gardens to eat, sitting peacefully by a placid lake bordered by tall trees, with the cathedral bells chiming the quarters.

June 21st: Today, the summer solstice, dawned grey and wet; I decided I had had enough of grey skies and longed for sunshine, although it seemed that today I wasn't going to get any. I managed to find a way out of town along secondary roads, crossed some fields, did an horrendous road–walk along the Lichfield–Ashbourne road, and eventually came to the Trent and Mersey canal. On the towpath my spirits rose on finding a milestone telling me it was twenty–nine miles to Shardlow, which I knew was just a few miles from my destination for the weekend. By road it was twenty–two miles to Ashbourne, a gateway to the Peak District.

I left the canal and crossed the river Trent, running high between its banks with flooded fields around, then climbed out of the valley and along more lanes to reach Fisher's Pit Farm, set on a hilltop. Fisher's Pit aimed to be a holiday attraction for families, with its population of rare breeds of farm animals and displays of vintage agricultural equipment, but today I was the only guest, and Mrs Aitkenhead told me with some regret that she and husband had decided to sell up and move to a smallholding, discouraged by the increasing problems of running a farm and business profitably.

The farm was in a beautiful situation, set well back from the road among fields and woods, with a view to the woods and hills of Cannock Chase the best part of ten miles away; the skies were clearing after a stormy day, but holding out little of promise for tomorrow. Mr Aitkenhead said that weather on the solstice holds the pattern for the remaining summer months, a variation on Saint Swithin. I had a substantial farm supper, more than I could comfortably eat, and watched from my window the light fading over the hills.

June 22nd: I left wearing windproofs in the face of a fierce wind and ominous looking clouds and walked into Abbot's Bromley, en route for Uttoxeter, where I would temporarily divert from my northward course to travel to Derby. I had found a promising–

looking line of red dot–dashes on the map leading in the right direction, and set off along a farm track, with thunder rumbling in the distance.

After a couple of miles the track turned to direct itself towards some farm buildings at the same time as the rain started and a farmer driving a Land Rover appeared accompanied by two unfriendly looking Alsations. I gave the farmer a good morning while looking cautiously towards the dogs, and received what I was coming to perceive as the standard greeting in these parts: 'Are you lost?', spoken in a broad Midland accent. I replied that I thought I was on a right of way, and was directed through a gate to 'the other side of the hedge'.

Fine, I thought, according to the map this is where the route should go. Only problem was, after two fields I came to a complete standstill. The map seemed clear about where the route went, across the corner of a wood and under power lines to join a lane by another farm. I could see the power lines ahead, but there seemed to be no way through. Uttering curses on map–makers and land–owners equally, I climbed to the top of the field through a flock of disconsolate–looking sheep, and came to a ditch with a rickety barbed–wire fence on its far side.

I managed to negotiate wire and ditch with nothing worse than a thorough wetting, and emerged into a huge field planted with waist–high cereal; I made my way along its edge for what seemed miles, until to my relief I came to a gate into the farm lane exactly where I expected it to be. It seemed reasonably clear that the track had fallen into disuse and been blocked and I resolved to report it to the Ramblers' Association. I sat in the hedge and had second breakfast.

As I walked along lanes towards Uttoxeter the landscape changed, wide fields giving way to steep hills, woodlands, and little dells with streams running through. On the summit of the last of the hills I looked down on to the wide valley of the river Dove and saw beyond it green hills rising above what I knew to be the Derbyshire Dales. I was very wet, cold, and needed food, and my ankle was aching remorselessly, but I started to sing 'afar crooning is pullin' me awa' as tak' I wi' my crummock to the road', Harry Lauder's old song about the Road to the Isles. I

61

rejoiced in the knowledge that, sore ankle, sore back, hostile farmers, bad weather notwithstanding I had Beachy Head, Bath and Birmingham behind me, and was more than halfway to Scotland.

Scarcely two hours later I was letting myself into the house lent to me by my sister Audrey and her husband John, absent on holiday in France. The transition had been so swift, by paytrain to Derby and taxi to the Derby suburb, that I felt quite bemused, and wandered round the house without even taking off my rucksack, anticipating spending four nights under the same roof after nine different lodgings since Cheltenham, and finding it difficult to decide what to do first.

Interlude

Life must be lived forwards but it can only be understood backwards.

Sören Kierkegaard

Derby has special associations for me, because it was here I learned about walking. We had moved from Southport in 1938, when I was fifteen, and I soon discovered the hills and dales of the Peak District.

Derby was quite different from genteel Southport; it was an industrial town becoming increasingly prosperous as England moved out of the depression of the twenties and early thirties, and with most of its population in work. The thing that really counted with me, though, was Derby's proximity to open countryside. The town was surprisingly compact in those days, lacking much of the urban sprawl which grew in the post–war years. I could walk out of the house, round the corner, into a field, and be on the banks of the river Derwent in fifteen minutes, while in the same time be able to cycle into town in the other direction. From there I could travel by bus to Ashbourne in a half hour, and reach the limestone dales by field footpaths.

The Peak District for me, as for so many people, thus became my principal recreation ground, to which I would return at every opportunity, and where I learned to find my way around the countryside, sometimes alone, sometimes with groups of friends. In those days the dress for walking was one's old clothes; my first walking footwear was a pair of shoes to which my father added hobnails, and my first rucksack looked exactly like a postman's sack. It was not until after the war when the market became flooded with all kinds of cheap army surplus goods that we began to use specialised gear.

It's over forty years since the demands of work took me to London, later to marry and rear a family, but the love for the countryside which developed during the Derby years has been one of the sustaining elements of my life.

Derby, then, was a good place to rest and take stock, and particularly good because of the atrocious weather; this was the week that the first day's play in the Wimbledon tennis tournament was washed out. A good time not to be on the road, but I began to be worried about how I would cope with the peat moors if things didn't improve.

On Sunday Dick arrived, bearing mail from home and fresh garden produce including my favourite strawberries. I disposed of ten days' sweaty gear, caught up with the news and wrote letters, and started to plan ahead. I had now walked 370 miles, some of them rather painful ones, but was becoming more confident of being able to keep walking. The only problem was that I could see myself running our of time. I had commitments that required my presence in London by the end of July and there was no way, at the rate at which I was going, that I could be at Cape Wrath before early August at best. I should just have to devise a Plan B. I could either walk on and stop when time ran out, or I could set my sights on another finishing destination, and make for there, leaving the rest of the route until next year.

I decided it would be neater to choose the latter course; I first thought of breaking off at Hadrian's Wall, which was a suffic- iently dramatic and easily identifiable place. Dick said yes, but he thought I ought to get to Scotland. This made sense; having walked through England this year, I would walk through Scotland in 1992. So I found the first Scottish town on my route which was called Newcastleton, and was three and a half miles inside the Scottish border, and decided that that was where I would stop. Having made the decision I settled down to enjoy three days of idleness, wondering vaguely if I would want to start up again, or if the motor would have run down. With few household chores to do and no other demands on my energies there was a real sense of time out and I revelled in sitting among the plants in the conservatory looking out at the rain, while Dick took the mower to the lawn in between showers and disappeared from time to time for runs in the surrounding countryside.

Wednesday came, Midsummer Day and Dick's seventieth birthday as it happened; celebrations would have to wait till later. We drove in ghastly traffic back to Uttoxeter station to pick up the route where I had left it. I waved goodbye and set off on the next stage of the journey.

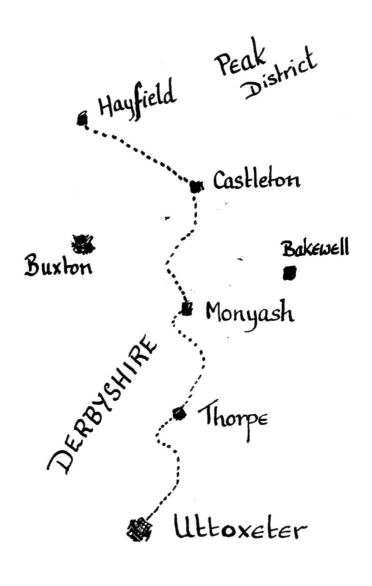

Peak District

Hayfield

Castleton

Buxton

Bakewell

Monyash

DERBYSHIRE

Thorpe

Uttoxeter

Uttoxeter to Hayfield

6: Heading for the Hills.

Wednesday 26th June: Before leaving Derby I discarded my 'softie' Brasher boots which showed no signs of wear after 370 miles of walking from Eastbourne, in favour of my heavier and well–worn in Hawkins Hillwalkers. There was something symbolic in the exchange, an anticipation of rough stuff to come, and I liked the way my feet settled into their change of footgear, an acceptance of the fact that the easy part was over.

I was aiming for the Pennine Way, the oldest national long–distance footpath, which, starting at Edale in Derbyshire, follows the high ground of the Pennines for over two hundred and fifty miles finally to arrive in Scotland at Kirk Yetholm. The Pennine Way is a paradox: it separates two of the most densely populated areas of the British Isles, but entails some of the country's roughest walking. People have been known to start the Pennine Way at Edale and abandon it at Crowden fifteen miles further on after acquaintance with the peat hags of Bleaklow.

Another aspect of the paradox is the popularity of the Pennine Way, with thousands of people walking it every year, so that it tends to be treated with less respect than it deserves; it is described scornfully as the Pennine Motorway. However, no one who has been on Kinder Scout or Bleaklow in severe weather is likely to treat the peat moors too lightly, or to go to them ill–equipped. I had been on Kinder Scout many times, but would still approach a solo expedition with due seriousness.

First I would cross the White Peak, the limestone plateau which covers much of south Derbyshire and Staffordshire; the rivers which dissect the plateau, Dove, Lathkill, Wye have carved for themselves the dramatic dales with their spectacular limestone cliffs which are a major attraction of the area. My particular love is the limestone uplands, rising to a height of a thousand feet and more, an ancient country crossed by packhorse tracks and with traces of the lead mines which, along with farming, once formed the main industry of the area. I love the austere greens of the fields, with their drystone walls so lovingly created in the past, a lonely landscape little changed over the centuries, with long views, where even in these days of mass tourism it is possible to find solitude. This was my country and I approached it with eagerness.

Uttoxeter had a busy market going on, and although there were lines of dots on my map marking a right of way starting from the station there was no trace of it on the ground. I wandered round the railway yard to try to find the footpath and finally gave up and walked along the main road trying not to smell the lorry fumes. I came to the river at Dovebridge, its waters swollen with all the rain, and looked down on a solitary fisherman under the arch of the bridge seeming to be oblivious to the roar of the traffic overhead. I left the road for the riverside, soon to be repelled by impenetrable thickets, so took to the lanes, now full of clover, honeysuckle, syringa, leading me towards those hills I had last seen from the other side of Uttoxeter.

The heavens opened again, with hail this time, and I didn't make it to the pub at Roston in time to escape a wetting. A farmer driving a Landrover stopped and asked if I would like a lift or whether I didn't mind the rain, so I explained that I couldn't accept lifts because I was walking to Scotland. Thinking about it, I realised that I really didn't mind the rain too much. I suppose that if one is determined to walk the length of the kingdom it wouldn't do much good to mind the weather. I was reminded of one very wet day walking with Dick in Wales when we were offered a lift by a passing motorist, and refused it because we were doing the a challenge walk called the Red Kite Trail. He looked disbelieving and commented, 'Whatever turns you on,' before driving off.

At the pub I had a hot roast beef sandwich and coffee and dried out, and by the time I left the sky was clearing and it suddenly turned into a fine afternoon, with blue sky and fluffy white clouds such as I hadn't seen it seemed for weeks. I crossed the main A52 road at Mayfield, becoming excited about walking into the limestone, and reached Okeover Deer Park, with cows and sheep grazing but no deer. I found my way along a footpath diverted to avoid the farm 'because of the fishing rights' explained a farm hand who was rounding up sheep, and descended to the riverside footpath through woods and fields, getting my boots well and truly muddy. I reached Caldwell Bridge, where I crossed into Derbyshire and climbed steeply up the hill to Thorpe, a neatly tailored village just settling down for the evening.

I had been in Thorpe many times in the past, but, after what must have been getting on for forty years' absence, I couldn't remember much about it, not even its position on a hilltop; the few people in the little village square were holiday visitors who didn't know the district either. Somewhere about here was the cottage where Mrs Chadwick used to brew limitless pots of tea, the place which was the natural halt for hundreds of ramblers on hundreds of Sundays in those far–off days when, for the Derby Nomads, Thorpe was the final halt on the way to Ashbourne. From there we used to occupy the rear seat of the bus, singing all the way home, the 'Manchester Rambler', and Cwm Rhondda, and 'we are the Nomads Rambling Club we ramble round from pub to pub'. Even in the age of the car, the Nomads still hire coaches for their organised walks; I hope they still sing.

I followed my nose, and came in a hundred yards or so to Broadlowash Lane and the guesthouse where I'd booked a bed. There was an old salvaged red telephone box in the garden. Later I climbed another steep hill to the farm where a sumptuous meal was waiting, homemade potato and onion soup, chicken in a good sauce, and blackcurrant crumble with cream, helped down by friendly conversation with the farmer's wife. I walked back in a cloudless evening with the hills crystal clear. I wrote: 'probably a bad–weather sign but I do so love the limestone hills; somehow a new element has entered the walk, and it's good to be on the way again'.

June 27th: In walker's Derbyshire it felt safe to say I'd walked from Beachy Head, and breakfast conversation, with two couples, one young, one my age, was all about walking and footpaths and country matters, and people saying 'I'd like to do that'. I felt lucky that I had means and strength to follow my own dream.

The day started fine and strenuous, with a climb to a thousand feet on to the plateau along a farm track, under more blue skies, wonderful familiar views across to the cone of Thorpe Cloud standing sentinel over the entrance to Dovedale. For all its over–use this is still a magic place. Soft green fields were overlaid with a geometric pattern of shining grey–white limestone walls, and little crags bordered small dry valleys descending to where I could see the road leading from Ashbourne to Buxton far below, the whole landscape gleaming in the sun.

I went down to cross the main road and climbed on to the embankment of the Tissington trail, one of the stretches of disused railway line which was closed in the Beeching era. The Peak Park Planning Board have imaginatively turned the line into a walkway and cycleway, and a number of nature reserves have been created along its length. The trail is one of the engineering marvels which nineteenth century railway builders wrought, climbing to a thousand feet through spectacularly beautiful countryside and with only gradual gradients has some of the characteristics of the drove roads I had been using.

There were more people about here, mostly in groups, walking and cycling including a group of about fifty Japanese cyclists coming in the opposite direction. All the lime–loving plants were in bloom, cowparsley, vetches, trefoils, ladies bedstraw,campions, buttercups and white marguerites. The may was still in bloom here, telling me that I was moving north. There were scores of little tame birds, chaffinches, bluetits, wagtails. Axe Edge, where the river Dove rises as a trickle out of the peat, came into view on the far horizon, flanked by the curiously shaped Chrome Hill.

Just as I was lunching the rain started in a repeat of yesterday's performance, with thunder and lightning for good measure, with no shelter and no pub in sight. Trudging on, I was overtaken by the lone walker I had last seen slumbering by the trackside, hat pulled down over his eyes, who complained that the rain had disturbed his afternoon nap. I directed a group of bedraggled young women walkers to Hartington Youth hostel, and, reaching the junction of the Tissington and High Peak trails at Parsley

Hay, paused to take stock. I had booked a bed at the Waterloo Inn at Taddington, but the rain showed no sign of abating and I decided to look for a closer refuge.

From the telephone box I was successful at the third attempt in getting a bed in Monyash, two miles down the road. I walked there in a deluge, hills blotted out and the thunder rumblng away. Mr Driscoll at Rock House was welcoming, took my wet clothes to dry and made me tea which I drank while watching one of the few matches which had so far been possible at Wimbledon. I began to worry about having to confront the peat moors in a few days' time.

Monyash is a former lead–mining village, like many in the White Peak. It is ancient, dating back to mediaeval times, and mentioned in the Domesday book. Only a stone's throw away is the path into Lathkill Dale, one of the most beautiful of the limestone dales, which starts unassumingly between low rounded green hills, and descends to where the river bubbles out of a low cave at the beginning of its descent in cataracts through lovely woods to join the River Wye. The village seemed to have escaped any attempts to turn it into a tourist attraction, and the Hobbit pub next door to Rock House was occupied only by locals. Despite the nice name there was a rather sad atmosphere and too many smokers, and I didn't linger after eating my plaice and salad.

June 28th: I breakfasted with a couple from Hampshire, doing walks from their car. I wrote: 'I didn't tell them about my walk, one gets a feeling about whether to or not, although they were very nice.' I crossed a stile out of the village and joined more green tracks across the high limestone moor. I came to the A6 road by the Waterloo Inn, in time to catch the only shower of the day, followed by a steady clearance, a strong north–west breeze, white clouds, sunshine, enough to put a spring in the step. The lanes were full of flowers again, including spotted orchis, and cows and sheep were feasting on sweet limestone grass. This was Bullock Smithy country, the route of a fifty–six mile challenge walk with a twenty–four hour time limit starting from Hazel Grove near Stockport and touching three counties. Dick and I had done this together three years ago.

I descended into Miller's Dale, where the Monsal Trail crosses the road over a high-arched viaduct. This is the old Bakewell–Buxton railway line of which John Ruskin, an early conservationist wrote 'any fool in Bakewell can be a fool in Buxton in a half hour'. I wonder if he would be pleased to see his hated line so well used by twentieth-century ramblers. I followed a small group of walkers to the Angler's Rest for lunch in the sun by the river, feeling at home.

It was steeply up the hill then, along more green roads with beautiful long sweeping views to Tideswell, dressed up for the festival of well dressing, then more limestone uplands opening up familiar views to gritstone country. I recited the names over like a litany: Froggatt and Stanage Edges drawn up for inspection on the Eastern horizon, with hang-gliders hovering over Hucklow Edge in the middle distance; to the north, the Mam Tor ridge with Lose Hill as its end stop, and Win Hill rising across the gap which holds river, road, and the railway track where runs the sprinter train between Sheffield and Manchester, now the sole surviving trans-Pennine railway in Derbyshire.

The crumbling shale of the Mam Tor ridge draws a line between the radiant limestone and the sombre dead peat of Kinder Scout, truly the Dark Peak. What is so satisfying for me about the Peak District is this juxtaposition between the light and the dark, the limestone with its hidden waters carving the spectacular dales and caverns, and the stark peat moors; nothing hidden about these, what you see is what you get. There is a unique complementarity about this contrast, as if it represents the light and dark of human nature.

I followed the road round the top of Bradwell Quarry, an infamous blot on the landscape, a whole hillside eaten away, descended steep Pindale and so came to Castleton, another return to the past. Here as a child I had first visited Derbyshire, taken there by a neighbour from Southport who had grown up in the Peak District. Castleton has probably always been a popular place for day outings, it is too near Sheffield not to be, but to me it was magic; I gazed spellbound at the the gash of Peak Cavern in the hillside above the village and never tired of watching the trout in the brown waters of the little stream. The countryside was a revelation; in comparison Southport was flat and uninteresting and I had had no idea that places like the Peak District existed.

Knowing that Castleton had a wealth of accommodation I had not bothered to book ahead, forgetting that it was Friday and people would be coming out for what looked like being a fine weekend. I quartered the village, to be greeted by 'no vacancies' signs sprouting outside every guesthouse. There was no network here to hand me on to and I began to wonder if I should have to walk on, with no certainty of accommodation in neighbouring villages Hope or Hayfield. Finally I remembered that Castleton has a large youth hostel, and deciding that it was any port in a storm made my way there.

'Youth' is a misnomer, for the YHA admits anyone of any age who is a member and can pay the modest accommodation charges. I hadn't stayed in a hostel since doing the Pennine Way but had taken the precaution of renewing my membership before leaving home. Castleton hostel is a rambling old listed building set in the centre of the village and when I entered seemed unnaturally quiet at a time when most hostellers are booking in. I soon learned the reason, that a large school party was expected, and realised that I could say good–bye to the prospect of a peaceful evening.

I'm sure that people in school parties don't intend to be a nuisance but when fifty or so children aged between seven and ten are gathered together and away from home it is inevitable that they get excited and thus, noisy, and there is nothing anyone can do about it. The school minibuses rolled up and I retreated to the 'quiet' room to look at maps and think about tomorrow. I wrote 'a good day today, I think yesterday's torpor was partly thundery weather. For the first time I actually felt fit, but I've decided to wait for suitable weather before tackling the Kinder–Bleaklow section.'

June 29th: The morning was fine, and I climbed up the Winnats Pass in company with many others on this sunny Saturday. Castleton has become almost a cul–de–sac since the road to Chapel–en–le–Frith across the slopes of Mam Tor was closed because of recurrent subsidence of the shale hillside. The alternative exit over the Winnats is too steep to take much motor traffic. On this sunny morning the pass was thronged with groups of cyclists, walkers, and sightseers around the entrance of the Speedwell cavern, one of the many caves for which Castleton is famous.

I climbed on to familiar ground, seeing Mam Tor ahead, and the little steep road leading to Edale along which I had cycled and walked so many times in the past, to the old youth hostel at Upper Booth, long closed in favour of the large building at Rowland Cote. Upper Booth had been a place for connoisseurs of the simple type hostel, a farm cottage with none of the frills people expect nowadays, with its own following of people who went there for the walking and didn't mind having to do their own cooking.

I climbed to the summit of the road, using steps which had been built to counter erosion of the shale hillside, and turned away from Edale, along Rushup Edge, a well-worn track and old packhorse road along the ridge strung between the limestone moors on the one side and the Edale valley on the other, at a height of about fifteen hundred feet. I went on happily, gloating in the well-remembered views and looking across the peat moors towards which I was heading. Coming in the opposite direction I met a number of parties of four young people, on Duke of Edinburgh award expeditions, I learned, all carrying large packs but cheerful and friendly. I descended to the road then took the track which leads over the western edge of the Kinder Scout moors and down to Roych Clough, to climb out again, and so to Hayfield. This is beautiful country, and the tracks, like most of those in the Peak District are clearly defined, but my stiff ankle didn't like the rough ground at all and I limped into the village feeling rather sorry for myself.

A new by-pass carrying the through road from Buxton to Glossop has given Hayfield a welcome respite from the plague of through traffic, although it is a pity that in its construction a corner of the village has been left stranded on its west side. The centre however remains untouched and it is an attractive place, busy this Saturday with day visitors and a cricket match on the green playing field in its centre. I booked in at my B&B, a fine large room, and thought that this might be a good place for a rest day if tomorrow's weather proved unpromising. I shopped for provisions for an evening meal, finding a whole food shop selling organic produce, and returned to watch TV and think about future plans.

June 30th: Heavy rain in the night and early morning decided me to wait another day; in any case, the next section would be the hardest of the whole walk before Scotland, and it made sense to start well rested. I liked Hayfield, too, finding it friendly and unpretentious; so I did essential chores and settled in for the day. Mr Collier–Johnson, the proprietor, showed me the original photographs of Benny Rothman and others on the mass trespass on Kinder Scout which started from Hayfield. Benny Rothman received a prison sentence for his participation, but now in his eighties is still working for access to the moors.

The rain stopped and I went out to look around Hayfield, now busy with dozens of walkers and some fell–runners, all heading up Kinder Road towards the moors, and leaving the village to less active Sunday visitors and locals. All the shops were open to make the most of Sunday trade. I bought a paper and went to find a seat by the river, a picturesque setting with the church opposite flaunting its over–sized clock, and the backs of pretty old three–storey houses reaching down to the water, the river making small cataracts as it flowed under the town bridge. Purple cranesbill was growing luxuriantly by the riverside and a family of ducks pottered busily around.

After a while I crossed the by–pass and went to look at the Sett Valley Trail. This used to be a branch railway line between New Mills and Hayfield, much used by ramblers until closed in 1970, now another popular traffic–free route for walkers, cyclists, and horse–riders, with an information centre on the site of Hayfield station. The Sett river was once an important source of water–power for cotton spinning and weaving from the time in the early industrial revolution when Hayfield was a prosperous small industrial town. Nowadays only one chimney still pours out smoke, from the mill manufacturing paper, not cotton. Most of Hayfield's working population now travel to Lancashire towns.

I went into a small restaurant, crowded with people eating

Sunday lunch, and was served by friendly staff with a huge omelette, more than I could comfortably eat, for what seemed a ridiculously low price. I realised that I was procrastinating and that tomorrow whatever the weather I would need to tackle what I knew would be one of the key sections of the walk. To penetrate north from here there was no reasonable alternative to the Pennine Way, and I was quite anxious about how my stiff ankle would perform among the peat hags. In the morning, July 1st as it happened, I begged wrapping paper from my friendly hostess and sent home some unwanted items of clothing in a rather do-or-die attempt to lighten my load; I braced myself for the coming trial by peat.

7: Perils of the peat

A stone's throw out on either hand
From that well-ordered road we tread,
And all the world is wild and strange.

[Yeats]

Monday July 1st: I had decided to leave out Kinder Scout this
time. I had done the Pennine Way once and didn't feel it
necessary to repeat it in full, it being more important to reach
Scotland in one piece; leaving out the section over Kinder
Downfall would shorten my day by about two miles of rough
country. So I set off up Kinder road, looking rather anxiously at
an overcast sky. After a mile I came to the carpark in the old
quarry by Bowden Bridge where walkers had gathered in 1932
for the mass trespass on Kinder Scout. I remembered having to
look out for keepers on early walks on Kinder and thought of the
debt owed to the campaigners for access to the countryside, who
had risked imprisonment and assault.

The tarmac road ended at the Kinder reservoir and I followed
the path up William Clough, to where it crosses the Pennine Way
at Ashop Head, at about 1600 feet above sea level. I was
surprised by the extent to which the track had deteriorated since
I had last used it some years ago; the banks of the river had
become badly eroded so that in places it was impossible to
follow the stream and I was forced to take to the hillside. This
was strenuous and time-consuming and I began to wonder if it
wouldn't have been more straightforward to have followed the
Pennine Way from the beginning. No matter; eventually I was
standing on the col at Ashop Head where the Pennine Way

Airton

Gargrave

Lothersdale

Keighley

Buckley Green

Colne

LANCASHIRE

WEST
YORKSHIRE

Hebden
Bridge

M62   Mankinholes

Halifax

Marsden

Forest
Farm

Saddleworth
Moor

Crowden

Glossop

Bleaklow Hill

Kinder Scout

Hayfield

descends from Kinder Scout after crossing the river above the Kinder Downfall. I took a picture of my first Pennine Way signpost and felt that I was now on a highway to the north.

It's hardly possible to explain to those unacquainted with peat moors what they are actually like. From a distance there is nothing in particular to warn of their character. Little can grow on peat because of the acid nature of the rotted vegetation of which it is composed, and this gives the moors the air of brooding darkness which they present in contrast with the shining limestone. The gradients, however, are easy, and from a distance the terrain looks smooth, with only the glint of water to inform the knowledgeable walker of the boot–drenching wetness which is owed to the sponge–like ability of peat to hold water, a characteristic explaining its popularity as a garden compost.

Mill Hill, which was my first objective on the Pennine Way, is trodden by the boots of countless walkers, but this doesn't help much. In this waterlogged landscape there are no firm paths, only soggy boot–flattened peat interrupted by pools and channels of water. It is impossible to walk in anything like a straight line because of the frequent diversions necessary for the walker to avoid sinking in above the boot–tops. On Mill Hill, and Featherbed Moss which follows, only a line of sparsely placed poles gives guidance as to direction.

To my shame, I forgot to keep an eye on these markers and went off course at one point, finding myself floundering among oozing peat hags (groughs), another delight of the peat moors. These are where the peat is intersected by drainage channels, sometimes to a considerable depth, worn away by erosion, sometimes down to the underlying grit, more often down to deeper sludge. You can't jump over the wider groughs, you have to descend and climb out and descend and climb out, getting covered in sludge in the process. It is easy to lose yourself among the groughs and I was relieved when a party of walkers appeared in the distance striding in what looked like the right direction; I changed my line of march to cross theirs and headed for the distant Snake road which joins Sheffield and Manchester. I arrived there feeling rather the worse for wear.

Once over the Snake there were signs of attempts to deal with erosion problems, an incongruous tarmac section for a half–mile, finishing abruptly in the fastnesses of the Devil's Dyke, where an intrusive notice exhorted the walker to keep to such paths as there were. I was now starting the crossing of Bleaklow, the aptly named area of peat moor which has an even more evil reputation than Kinder Scout, for the depth and glutinosity of its peat hags. I approached this as one does the crux on a rock climb. At first the going was fairly straightforward; the path followed the bottom of the Devil's Dyke, mainly on firm sand and climbed steadily to reach the place at Hern Clough where only a few yards separate streams flowing eastward to the North Sea and west–ward to the Irish Sea. I was overtaken by a party of young backpackers, and followed them out of the watercourse and on to the bare moor, as they vanished out of sight.

I had been here before, on the trackless plateau of Bleaklow, but it didn't seem to help; there was nothing to be seen but acres of dark peat sparsely covered in vegetation, low ridges sweeping away on every side with no recognisable features or landmarks. While I was trying to check my direction, what I had most feared happened; the cloud which had been lurking to the west for most of the day decided to close in. It happened with disconcerting suddenness; one moment I was looking across the desolate moor, the next I was engulfed in a blanket of thick wet cloud. Hastily putting on waterproofs I considered my position.

I knew that somewhere to the north was the cairn on Bleaklow summit whence I could take a bearing and set a course to take me down into Longdendale. I knew it wasn't far and once at the cairn I would have no further navigation problems but for a moment I panicked. I knew that it wasn't safe to trust such footprints in the peat as there were; Wainwright warns that the people making them may be lost too!

'Trust the compass,' I said sternly to myself, (what would Wainwright have done, he never carried one?) I set a bearing and steered by it and as the mist thinned relaxed as I saw the cairn of Bleaklow Head looming through the murk. From there it really was downhill all the way. I steered a course to a small stream and followed it as it left the peat and started to descend. Below me a view opened out of hills enfolding a valley and far below the Torside Reservoir, with hills rising on its far side. It was a long, long descent along a path now well–defined but twisting and turning along the hillside as if reluctant to arrive in the valley. My pace became progressively slower as the ground steepened on the final descent to the road.

For a while the clouds cleared and the views were beautiful, with the declining sun turning the waters of the reservoir to gold and the hills enfolding the valley looking deceptively green and benign. A couple overtook me, on their first day of the Pennine Way, but I soon fell behind. I trudged along the path through pinewoods, with the rain starting again, and was glad to see the shape of the hostel on the hillside opposite.

Out of not wanting to tempt providence I hadn't booked ahead, but Crowden hostel had space, although I was too late for supper. To enter the hostel was like going back thirteen years in time, when young son Robert and I, after our first Pennine Way day, had arrived, in the rain as of now. The hostel itself is rather an impersonal, businesslike institution, with strict rules about removing muddy boots and gear. There was the same deep sink for rinsing off peat–stained gaiters and the wet tropical heat of the drying room. There is nevertheless a unique atmosphere, arising from the knowledge that most people who enter the hostel's portals are survivors of the peat, and there is a fellow–feeling related to the shared hardships of the day.

I telephoned home to report my successful assault on Bleaklow, then bought soup and tinned peaches from the store, and ate supper in the members' kitchen, in the company of the young walkers I had last seen on Bleaklow. There was a multinational clientele, including three very large Americans and some French cyclists. A Yorkshireman, seeing my battered copy of Wainwright, asked if it was any easier the second time round; I didn't think so, in fact was feeling surprised at how tough it had been. It is a curious fact that memory is selective in how it deals with the past; you know that you've done it and you remember what it was like, except for the pain. I'm sure there was more pain this time; after all, I was thirteen years older!

July 2nd: I had decided to chicken out of following the Pennine Way over notorious Black Hill, with more unfavourable weather forecast so set off for a horrendous mile along the A628 road to Woodhead, with juggernauts breathing down my neck; it was more peaceful on the thousand–foot climb to Holme Moss, of the television tower landmark. Holme Moss is famed as a hill–climb on national cycling events, the Tour of Britain and Milk Race among them. Today the summit was shrouded in cold mist as I walked from Lancashire into West Yorkshire, then down the hill into the village of Holme. From here a little road led to Digley, a peaceful spot where I lunched by the reservoir in sunshine before making my way back to rejoin the Pennine Way at Wessenden.

Near Wessenden the water board was at work with heavy earth–moving equipment and had diverted the Pennine Way across the reservoir dam. I descended to Marsden past banks of rhododendrons to where I was to spend the night about a mile outside the town and well off route. Marsden struck me as on a past visit as a rather dour town, with moors rising steeply above, road, river and railway running along the valley, fronted by many–windowed mills for all the world like a Lowry painting. I watched an unfavourable weather forecast and realised again that the Pennine Way was no doddle for someone with a dodgy ankle. Tomorrow I had a fifteen mile walk to the Calder valley.

July 3rd: The nice people I had breakfast with 'I'd love to do a long walk like you're doing' gave me a lift back into Marsden. They were driving home to Leeds after seeing a married daughter. It was just starting to rain, steadily as if it had all day to do it in and was in no hurry to stop. I waited for the bus up the hill to Standedge cutting and the Pennine Way. Here it was impossible to see across the road, and crossing it was hazardous with heavy traffic thundering by. I groped along the verge to find the Pennine Way signpost, and looked rather despondently at the track rising into the mist. I was filled with what we used to call disclinitis at the thought of spending the following six or so hours in this murk, but took tentative steps along the track for a hundred yards or so before deciding that it might be better to wait for a clearance.

I walked back down the road for a quarter mile to find the pub about to open, and ordered coffee and fish and chips, while a radio played, 'raindrops keep falling on my head.' I tried to decide what to do. It was already afternoon, and if I went on there was nowhere to stay until Mankinholes Youth Hostel in fifteen miles; I was unsure whether even if the weather improved I could get there before dark. I was equally reluctant to go back to Marsden and to repeat the morning's operation. And that is how I came to find Forest Farm, and to meet May Fussey.

I consulted my accommodation lists, and used the pub telephone to ring the farm, waited until the pub closed on me and just two other customers, then walked a half mile or so down a side road with the clouds thinning as I descended. The farm was a low stone building opposite, of all things, a golf course on the hillside, where a few people were playing in the wet mist and minimal visibility.

May Fussey greeted me warmly and I immediately felt at home, offered bath, tea, and food. I was soon ensconced in the comfortable sitting room drinking tea and watching Boris Becker defeat Bergstrom in an exciting singles match. I did my usual routine of checking out distances and progress, feeling that I seemed to be spending too much time on this part of the walk, but was reassured in finding that despite being only one and a half miles further along the Pennine Way than when I left Marsden I would without any further delays reach Gargrave by the weekend, where I had arranged a rendezvous. May Fussey was used to end–to–end walkers and I was thrilled to find in the visitor's book that Ron Scholes had stayed there. I had corresponded with Ron about his walk from Cape Wrath to Land's End two summers earlier after his retirement from teaching. Here was evidence that it was possible.

July 4th: I slept more soundly that night than I had   since leaving home and left next morning feeling valued and cared for. The cloud was still low over Standedge but at least the rain had stopped and I felt optimistic that it might clear. The way unfolded itself, now with an occasional glimpse through the murk of industrial Lancashire. It was nice to be on the firm footing of the gritstone edges and my spirits rose. Soon a lark began to sing, a curtain–raiser to the lifting of the mist.

There was a mucky stretch to follow, the crossing of the

horribly littered A672 road, with a layby piled high with rubbish, a look down from the footbridge on to speeding traffic on the M62, then the horror of Redmires, a short section this compared with Bleaklow, but with a veritable Slough of Despond where the path crossed its low points; the few places where pieces of corrugated plastic had been placed to bridge the chasms served only to emphasise the desolation. Tolkien must have had such places in mind when he described the Dead Marshes before Mordor.

Thankfully I escaped to firmer ground on Blackstone Edge, with the boisterous east wind trying to blow me away. Views opened out again, the Lancashire towns to the west, and ahead to the moors above Calderdale. More people appeared, some backpackers, a couple of fell–runners, and a man on horseback. I could see the White House pub on the road below for a half hour before reaching it, but found I was too late for coffee, and had to settle for shandy and crisps, since they'd also finished serving food.

There was another battering to follow; the wind was whipping up the waves on the line of reservoirs, Blackstone, Light Hazzles and Warland. The reservoir retaining walls were good protection against the blast, then every so often the wind would find a gap to roar through. It was a wild scene, with the clouds hurtling by, and the mist still lurking over the bare moors to the front. Whoever coined the word 'wuthering' knew what they were talking about.

Once I was away from the water and out on the open moor the wind moderated. I had my first glimpse of Stoodley Pike, the monument commemorating the peace of Ghent in 1814 which commands the view over Calderdale. Stoodley Pike is a famous landmark, dominating the whole of the Calder valley and visible for miles around. The tower took a long time to come closer; I passed a sign saying BUS STOP which must have been three miles or more from the nearest road, and before reaching the monument's foot took the flagged path down to Mankinholes and the youth hostel, another return to the past. Robert and I had stayed here in 1978, with a whole cohort of Pennine Way walkers such as I hadn't seen this time round.

There was a different warden and the old house was obviously feeling its age; there was a school party too, but there was a friendly feel about the place, and it looked as though I would have a room to myself, one of the privileges of age.

At dinner I shared a table with four army personnel, who were doing a sponsored walk for mental handicap north to south along the Pennine Way, carrying packs and doing about double my stages. I was impressed by their organisation, with two back-up vehicles and one of their number carrying a portfolio with the expedition planned in meticulous detail. They were friendly and intelligent and I was touched to observe how the boys in the school party, aged only seven or so, were fascinated by having them around; it was clear that the armed forces were regarded as desirable role models, perhaps hardly surprising so soon after the Gulf War.

There was a magnificent red and orange sunset, with the wind still blowing fiercely, but a good weather forecast for the morrow.

July 5th: I abandoned the Pennine Way to walk into Hebden Bridge along a well-graded bridleway starting just along the road from the hostel. The track took me along the slopes of the moor below Stoodley Pike, with views to the Calder valley below, through gates and over streams. From afar I saw a fell-runner silhouetted against the horizon and loping along the Pennine Way, and thought how easy he was making it look, while I was toiling along under my load. I descended steeply to the road, looking down on toy-like traffic speeding along the narrow valley. In Hebden Bridge I was successful in finding bank, an information centre, and a shop to sell me batteries for my radio, all within the same hundred yards in the High Street.

Calderdale's slopes are dauntingly steep, and I laboured up the hill to Heptonstall, on to National Trust land, Hardcastle Crags, and people sunbathing, with the sun now beating down. I rejoined the Pennine Way by the Packhorse Inn, where the route left the moorland road. I lay by the side of the track eating lunch and feeling too hot. Off to Walshaw Dean Reservoir, then, in the teeth of another blustery wind, meeting day and Pennine Way walkers coming in the opposite direction. There were more path improvements on Withens heights, but there was blue sky and the wind was keeping it cool. At Top Withens a couple were trying to discourage some importunate sheep who were filching sandwiches and obviously unused to being repelled.

This is Bronte country and the signposts and waymarks around this area now include directions in the Japanese language for the numerous Japanese tourists who come to see the Haworth home of the Bronte sisters. I saw no Orientals today, but on this fine day the many local footpaths were busy. The last time I was here it was wet, and Robert and I had still ten miles to go to our night's lodging. I had given myself an easy day.

I walked for a while with a young backpacker, talking about long-distance walking. 'Are you doing all the Pennine Way?' he asked. 'Well, no, but...' I still wasn't sure what I was doing; I must think of a non-committal sort of answer to the question. My companion left me to camp at the next farm, and I took a right-angled turn, and descended a green lane to find myself opposite Buckley Green where I was to spend the night. The fine day had been a morale-raiser after the mostly grey skies of the past week, and it was nice to be in a quiet farmhouse after the hubbub of Mankinholes. I ate strawberries and cream after chicken for supper, and caught up on the news. In the tennis Stefan Edberg, I learned, had lost to an unknown called Stich, who was later to win the championship.

July 6th: The morning was unbelievably sultry after the freshness of yesterday, and I was soon sweating as I passed Ponden Hall and climbed up the steep hillside on to Ickornshaw Moor. This is a heather moor, with negligible peat, and the path well marked by cairns, but I was surprised at the intricacy of the route-finding once I was descending towards Cowling. Thunder was rumbling away in the distance, and the air full of electricity. I came to a valley head where a waterfall descends steeply to Lumb Head Beck, and stopped to put on a cagoule as a few heavy spots of rain fell. A walker hurried past, not responding to my greeting, and obviously in a hurry to be off the moor. There were sheep here, agitated by the threat of the oncoming storm, running around aimlessly.

Sheep are sensitive to changes in the weather. I remembered

being in a Scottish bothy in the Ben Nevis area. It had turned increasingly sultry as the evening wore on and we looked out to see a small group of sheep, no more than three or four, stepping purposefully down the track towards lower ground – and wondered what they were doing. We were soon to find out; there followed a violent thunderstorm, which went on all night, with torrential rain in which the river changed its course. After a while we heard a loud grinding noise from the hillside, sounding as if a bulldozer were at work; huge boulders dislodged by the flash flood were being swept down the river – we were thankful to be under a watertight roof.

Next morning there was a magical clearance, with the mountains crystal clear under sparkling blue skies. Sure enough, we saw the same group of sheep returning up the track looking justifiably smug in having survived the storm. I have never since regarded sheep as lacking in intelligence.

I reached the stile leading on to the road at Cowling as the rain started in earnest, and as a group of three walkers came up behind me. In the deluge we huddled under a rather inadequate hawthorn tree until the worst of the downpour was over, then made a dash for the pub just a hundred yards along the road. The four of us lunched together; they were two primary school teachers from Leicester and a final year student. It was a pleasant interlude, with no pressure of time, as I was only a few miles away from my night's destination at Lothersdale.

Climbing out of Cowling meant crossing the grain of the country, in and out of steep wooded valleys. The rain had stopped, and it was becoming breathtakingly hot, with the humidity ridiculously high, like being in a Turkish bath, so I sweated and struggled as I climbed and descended and climbed again to reach Woodhead Farm.

Memories came flooding back. It was here in 1978 that Rob and I had arrived at nightfall after a twenty–two–mile day, Rob limping badly with a strained foot. There was a full house, a party of pony–trekkers, at least a half–dozen other Pennine Way walkers, and campers in the field below the house. Mrs Burnop, I learned later, never turned anyone away, and seemed to cope without fuss with all the cooking and organisation. Everyone was so sympathetic to Rob, at thirteen the youngest of the party by far, that I felt something of a tyrant for urging him on. Today, the farmhouse was quiet and deserted; I had read with sadness of Mrs Burnop's death the previous year, and the farm was now part of a consortium managed from elsewhere. There would be no more B&B at Woodhead but I knew that many people like myself would have fond memories of climbing the hill and finding the farm's low–lying buildings right on the Pennine Way.

I went on and stopped at the top of the hill before descending into Lothersdale, to look down on the picturesque group of grey houses nestling in the valley, topped by the tall chimney which used to be a textile mill. After the sombre moors it was delightful to rest the eyes upon this pastoral landscape. There was a valedictory air about today, because tomorrow would be the last day on which I would be walking by myself; after tomorrow, and until I reached Scotland I would have companions, and although I should enjoy this I would also miss the challenge of being dependent on my own resources. I would be leaving the Pennine Way for a time, and would miss the comradeship of other long distance walkers. So I spent a few moments thinking about how the past weeks had been and how I had enjoyed my time out of the everyday world.

I came to the village street, with people enjoying the unaccustomed warmth – the temperature must have been in the eighties. A mother was scolding her son for wearing too many clothes on 'the hottest day of the year'. I went on to find my B&B, next to the pub as I had been informed. Burlington House was an imposing–looking building built in blocks of local stone; I thought it might have once housed a manager of the textile mill across the road. I couldn't open the front gate so went around to the back door, the 'tradesmen's entrance' said Mrs Wood, who greeted me. In addition to tea and bath, Mrs Wood offered to put my unspeakably sweaty clothes in the washing machine, an offer gratefully accepted. I was used to having socks dried, but no one had ever before done my washing!

There is absolutely no point on a long distance walk in carrying more than a single change of clothes; in a rucksack things are likely to become almost as travel–stained as if worn; I had therefore hitherto relied upon doing my own washing on rest days. After Bleaklow and Ickornshaw Moor, with no rest day immediately in sight, it was good to contemplate once more being nice to know.

I went along the road to telephone, then to the Hare and Hounds pub to eat, a huge pizza, of which I had to save a quarter for the morrow's lunch. I was joined by my friends from Cowling, who were camping at the farm up the road, and we sat outside watching the light fade over the hills and talking of walking and travel. I went back to Burlington House to watch the news and weather to find that Steffi Graf had gained the women's championship at Wimbledon, and the West Indies looked like winning the third Test. I thought what a nice place Lothersdale was, a place to linger, as Wainwright wrote; I felt lucky in being here for what felt like an ending.

Mrs Wood provided a magnificent breakfast, starting with melon, and an enormous plate of eggs and bacon with all the accompaniments, and came to talk about Lothersdale and about my walk, and the book I hoped to write. .

July 7th: It was a brilliantly sunny morning, as I climbed over the heather moor to reach Pinhaw Beacon, a surprising little summit with an extensive view north over the green valley of the Aire river to the limestone hills above Malham. I was on course for the Yorkshire Dales leaving the peat behind for a while, another stage of the walk completed.

I crossed a road and took the lane opposite, descending steadily. A half-grown lamb ran from a field in front of me, and preceded me down the road, looking back anxiously from time to time, and trying unsuccessfully to find a way back into its field out of my way. So we went on, with me trying to appear harmless, and the lamb unwilling to trust me sufficiently to return the way it had come. In the distance I heard plaintive bleating coming from the mother sheep. After half a mile of this the lamb must have decided that it would prefer to face me rather than risk the wrath of its parent, so took its courage in all four feet, drew itself up, and scampered past me, all legs extended like a racehorse. I felt relieved, as I had wondered if I would have a lamb for companion for the rest of the walk.

As I descended I walked into summer from the half–life of the bare moors. Wild roses, clover, marguerites – and nettles – were growing in the hedgerows, while the elder was in scented bloom. The promised heatwave still seemed as far away as ever, it now clouding over and the afternoon wind getting up. I walked along the road to Gargrave; this was cycling country, with groups of brightly clad people riding sports cycles swooping down hills and round corners.

I crossed the Aire river, and found the town busy with more cyclists, walkers, and day visitors. I found the Dalesman cafe on the corner of West Street looking just as it had thirteen years ago, and went in to drink tea and eat cheese on toast. The friendly proprietress wanted to know what I was doing, and brought the old Pennine Way book so that I could find our entry of August 1st 1978, then proceeded to tell the rest of the customers that I'd walked from Beachy Head!

I walked up the lane, and, forsaking the Pennine Way, took the bridleway to Bell Busk, a stony track hard on the feet in the hot afternoon, climbing the hillside then descending to cross the river Aire again just where the minor road to Malham enters the York-shire dales National Park. I went on down the road to Airton, in the face of a stream of traffic, with little room for foot travellers.

At Airton I was in the heart of limestone country, smooth green hills, drystone walls and sheep grazing. I walked to the far end of the village, to Lindon House where I had arranged a rendezvous, and booked in, to be followed shortly by Audrey and John Timmins, arrived by car from Derby. It was a joyful re–union, with much news to exchange, and plans to make for the next stage of the walk. We ate Dales roast lamb, drank the first wine I'd had since Derby, and socialised with the other couple staying in the house, then watched a rather adverse weather forecast.

Tomorrow John was returning to Derby while Audrey would walk with me for the week. Audrey and I had done much of our early walking together, and had shared memories of adventures in the Lakeland hills and of a memorable trip to France soon after the end of the war. Audrey was a seasoned walker, having with John done many of the well–known long distance walks including a double completion of the Pennine Way from south to north and north to south. I was looking forward to our time together.

8: Across the Dales

*'We must certainly acknowledge that solitude is
a fine thing; but it is a pleasure to have someone
who can answer, and to whom we can say, from
time to time, that solitude is a fine thing.'*
[Honoré de Balzac]

Monday July 8th: We made a quick getaway, driven by John to
the village where we crossed the river and climbed the steep road
into Calton, then ascended Fosse Gill to find the high bridleway
which leads over limestone moor to join the road from Malham
near Gordale Scar. John came with us to the top of the hill then
jogged back to drive the car with most of our luggage round to
Malham and give us the pleasure of walking without packs for
a while. It was open country, with wide views over the Craven
hills, and to the bulk of Fountains Fell beyond. The track led on
to the moor, crossed a shallow valley, and followed a friendly
wall. From afar we saw John waiting for us at the high point
where Weets Cross marks four township boundaries.

We went on to meet the end of the road above Malham where
John left us to drive back to Derby, while Audrey and I set off
along Mastiles Lane on the crossing from Airedale to Wharfedale, the first of a number of crossings between dales that we
were to do in the next few days.

Mastiles Lane, or 'Gate', is an ancient monastic road, used
many centuries before the advent of motor transport. It at one
time formed a major trade route, at least dating from the twelfth
century, linking Fountains Abbey near Ripon with the Cistercian
abbey at Kilnsey, and westwards to extensive estates in the Lake
District. Like many such green roads Mastiles Lane dates from
prehistory and also has Roman connections, with the site of a

Kirkland

Slakes

Penrith

Appleby

Brough

Kirkby Stephen

Settle–Carlisle Railway

Moorcock Inn

Apperset

Hawes

Gayle

Raisgill

Kettlewell

Settle

Malham

Airton

camp noted just above Gordale Scar. It was an exhilarating walk over the high moor on this brooding grey overcast morning, with only the sheep for company, and a lapwing calling, the green track easy beneath our feet, the lane striding ahead between stone walls, and mounting the hillside scattered with limestone scars.

We came to the summit of the moor and descended on a pain- fully rough track, past a quarry entrance, arriving with the rain in Kilnsey village. Once again pub and rain happened together, and here was the Tennant Arms at the foot of the hill. The pub was crowded with car–borne customers; not a walker's pub, we decided, but we were able to have coffee, and set off again along the road under Kilnsey Crag; this imposing cliff, formed in the Ice Age by a glacier grinding its way down Wharfedale, is close enough to the road running along the valley to be a tourist attraction. Today a group of brightly–clad climbers was shelter- ing under the overhang, waiting for the rain to stop.

We crossed water–meadows to Conistone Bridge, with the rain becoming more determined, and in the absence of cover lunched by the village green on the memorial seat to Walter Hebden 1988. The landscape was becoming obscured beneath a veil of rain, and the minor road we took following the course of the river was running with water. Kettlewell came in due course, and we followed direction signs to find our B&B in a row of cottages opposite the police station, thankful to be in the dry. Over tea we watched England's last wicket stand in the Trent Bridge test until bad light stopped play.

At the Bluebell Inn which was crowded with holiday visitors we had to wait an hour for our home–made curry, which was delectable when it arrived, full of all sorts of goodies. Looking in my diary I found that, undetected, I had today passed the five hundred mile mark, which was I estimated just about halfway to Cape Wrath. The four hundredth mile had been reached some- where between Monyash and Castleton.

July 9th: The bad weather continued through the night, wind and rain battering the windows, good to be under cover. We break- fasted with a friendly Yorkshire couple doing day walks, and about to take off for Buckden Pike. Audrey, out of extensive experience of walking in the Dales, questioned them closely:

'Do you have a compass?'

'No'

'An Ordnance Survey map?'

'No.'

Audrey tut–tutted on learning that they relied on a book of local walks and gave a little lecture about going properly equipped to the hills. We had both served our apprenticeships in hill–walking in Derbyshire and I knew that I would feel inadequately dressed on an excursion without map and compass.

We walked through the village and crossed a stile on to the riverside pointing to the Dalesway, an eighty–mile long distance footpath starting in Ilkley and following some of the most beautiful of the Yorkshire Dales to finish in Bowness–in–Windermere in the Lake District. Despite its name the Dalesway is more than a riverside path, having crossings over high moor-land to Ribblesdale and hence to Dentdale. We were to follow the Dalesway only as it led to Upper Wharfedale, and set off beside the river, in brown spate, with the path flooded in places, and water–fowl struggling to hold their own against the strong current.

It was easy walking through fields and over stiles; we met other parties, people doing the length of the Dalesway, which is well waymarked and has accommodation in camping barns as well as the ubiquitous B&B. We crossed parkland to Buckden village where we sat out a heavy shower having tea and scones in the tea–shop behind the pub, then walked on through woods and more flowery fields with marsh marigolds and foxgloves.

We came to the packhorse bridge at Hubberholme, on another of the local drove roads, and found a seat by the river to eat cheese and biscuits and chocolate. Across the road sheep were being brought in for the shearing, and the air was full of the cries of lambs protesting at being separated from their mothers, a sound which was to become increasingly familiar over the coming week. Small birds came to eat our crumbs, swallows flew by and jackdaws scolded, and a young oyster catcher stood on a rock watching us, but not daring to come close enough for a photograph. The river had subsided from its early turbulence and was now running clear. With a short afternoon's walk ahead of us we followed the river, climbed a low knoll, then descended into green meadows brightly carpeted with flowers, the river accompanying us in small falls and cataracts interspersed with dark pools, and the sky clearing in the north–west wind.

At Yockenthwaite, where the ancient route over Horsehead Pass from Halton Gill which once carried traffic to markets at Askrigg and Hawes crosses the Wharfe we turned down the unfenced road to High Raisgill where we were to spend the night. This was a sixteenth–century farmhouse set in an old–fashioned garden full of summer flowers. After the bustle of Kettlewell this was a peaceful place to end the day; we dined on fresh trout, and afterwards sat in the comfortable sitting–room to write up log and postcards.

Mrs Middleton, our hostess, talked about how few visitors there were in the area, blaming this on a combination of bad weather and recession. Nice from the point of view of people like me who enjoy solitude, but not so good for local residents who depend on supplementing their income from the tourist trade.

July 10th: We left on a fine warm morning, with broken cloud, and the river now a gently flowing stream. At Beckermonds the Wharfe vanishes from the map to be rechristened, (if that is the right word) the Oughtershaw Beck, which has descended from its source high among the mosses of Cam Fell.

There is no right of way along the west bank of the Oughter-shaw Beck so we walked along the narrow Hawes road for a mile, untroubled by traffic. At the hamlet of Oughtershaw we turned on to a stony lane beside the river. The valley broadened out as the scenery became progressively bleaker and the valley lonelier; gone were the green woods and enfolding slopes, and in their place were marshy sedge grass and bare moorland, crossed by a patchwork of stone walls. We passed Nethergill Farm, (now, we noticed, offering accommodation), and as the path became narrower and less defined, came to the isolated farm of Swarthgill, with its wind–breaking barrier of tall trees visible from afar.

The Dalesway continues to follow the course of the stream to Cam Houses, and finally climbs to join the Pennine Way; at this point Cam High Road is reached, yet another upland highway owing its origin to the Romans, who used it to establish military communications throughout the region. We were aiming to cut off a corner to join Cam High Road earlier in its course, with Hawes as our objective, so a half-mile further up the valley we left the Dalesway to climb steeply up the eastern hillside. There is no right of way shown on the map here but no obstacles to progress in the way of fences, many of the stone walls having long collapsed in the absence, perhaps, of any need of enclosures on this open hillside.

It was a steep climb of about two hundred metres over ankle-wrenching grassy tussocks, but was soon over, and we emerged on to an upland scattered with limestone outcrops and a few hundred yards later reached the narrow unfenced tarmac road. Here we stopped to pick out through the mists the shapes of the Three Peaks, Ingleborough, Pen-y-Ghent and Whernside, the dominant limestone summits of the Yorkshire Dales. A half-mile road walk brought us to the Pennine Way at Kidhow Gate, the point where the route leaves Cam High Road to descend to Hawes. Kidhow Gate, marking a watershed of three river systems, has the feeling of being a universal meeting place; you never know who you might find here, and we paused to take photographs and to exchange greetings with other Pennine Way walkers.

We turned down the track signed Hawes 5 miles, and soon stopped to rest and eat lunch in a hollow sheltered from the wind and to enjoy some rare warmth, then later to stroll down to Gayle along the green track in idyllic conditions, with the views becoming sharper, and the valleys of Wensleydale spread below for our delectation. In the solitude it was difficult to believe that this was the Pennine Way, criticised by some as being like a regimented route-march.

We reached Gayle through field footpaths and walked through the village to find our night's lodging at Gayle Laithe, an old house a stone's throw from the fast-flowing Duerley Beck which flows down to join the river Ure at Hawes; today we had made a major crossing from Wharfedale.

We did some rather desperate and unsuccessful telephoning in the attempt to find accommodation at Garsdale Head, our tomorrow's objective. In the end we gave up and booked beds for two nights in Kirkby Stephen, deciding to use public transport to shuttle us from Garsdale Head for the first night.

In Hawes, a short walk across the field by the river, we found a choice of eating places, settling for good Yorkshire ham at the Board Inn, an improvement on the hostel fare I remembered from 1978. Our spirits were raised by the discovery that we would be able to reach Kirkby Stephen by train from Garsdale Head. We thought Hawes a lively place with a late opening Spa supermarket where we were able to replenish our stores of goodies for the march.

July 11th: Over breakfast we begged from fellow guests a copy of the timetable for the Carlisle–Settle railway; at the same time Audrey's revelation that I had walked from Beachy Head turned out to be one of those conversation–stopping pronouncements which we had come to recognise by the blank faces and response of 'Oh really'.

We walked across fields to reach the main Sedbergh road for a mile roadwalk to Apperset, where we took to the bank of the river Ure, which we were to follow towards its source high on the Mallerstang moors. This was a transformation from the austere Upper Wharfe, with steep wooded banks at first forcing foot travellers out on to the hillside. We found a rudimentary path with a shepherd rounding up his flock in the distance; we crossed some challenging stiles and climbed up the valley to Mossdale Head, the river becoming more attenuated as we went. The valley became more pronounced, with the bulk of Whernside appearing to the west like a recumbent beast. We crossed some cultivated fields and descended to cross the road by a farm and take the field path opposite, climbimg the hillside to find another line of stiles across moorland.

The river fell below us, turning into a mountain beck, its sheltering trees gone. A group of lambs scampered up to Audrey, allowing her to pet them and be photographed. It was becoming swelteringly hot, and we stopped in the shelter of a hill plantation to cool off, only to to be attacked by an assortment of stinging beasties, midges, clegs and mosquitoes, Audrey in shorts bearing the brunt of the onslaught. We climbed again to the hill farm at Yore House to join the farm track to the road and Garsdale Head. This had been an interesting and enjoyable walk, full of variety, with unexpected views of the hills.

The Moorcock, an old coaching inn, set on the junction of the hill road leading to Kirkby Stephen, was open for business, and we sat outside lunching in the sun. It was becoming clear that we could have found lodging at Garsdale Head, at the inn or at one of two private houses offering bed and breakfast, but we decided to continue with our original plan of heading for Kirkby Stephen, so walked along the road and up the hill to Garsdale Head station to catch the afternoon sprinter train.

The railway, which crosses some of the wildest sections of the Yorkshire moors, with spectacular views, has for a number of years been under threat of closure, only saved by the activities of pressure groups. We were pleased to find that when it arrived the train was crowded, mostly with holiday–makers, auguring well for the railway's future. The train laboured up the hill to Aisgill Head, at 364 metres the railway's highest point, coming out of a tunnel to a view of Wild Boar Fell windswept and formidable beneath its afternoon cloud cover. Once over the watershed we rattled down the valley to Kirkby Stephen station. The station, it turned out, was one and a half rather unpleasant miles from the town, along a main road without pavement with lorries thunder-ing by, so it was with some relief that we came into town to find our B&B in Fletcher House, next to the youth hostel, and non-smoking, as our hostess had taken pains to point out!

It was another house where I felt immediately at home, look-ing out on to the High Street as it must have for a century or more; inside were huge rooms furnished to match the house's size, with antiques and original paintings. Happily we took possession of a large twin room and unpacked our rucksacks secure in the knowledge that tomorrow we should be able to walk carrying less weight. It felt like having a rest day, just at the right time.

Kirkby Stephen was full of people with rucksacks; this is a staging post, where Wainwright's Coast to Coast walk from St Bees' Head in the Lake District to Robin Hood's Bay in North

Yorkshire leaves Cumbria to head across the Pennines. We walked into town to eat at the Pennine Hotel, also busy with walkers, feeling rather smug that we were making our own route raher than relying on someone else's.

July 12th: At breakfast there were tales of woe from resident coast–to–coasters with sore feet and too–heavy packs. Outside people were loading up mini–buses to carry luggage to the next stage of the Coast–to–Coast; this way of doing long–distance walks is becoming increasingly popular, with walkers being freed from the additional effort entailed in carrying heavy loads, and local carriers are finding welcome income from ferrying luggage.

We left by bus, reluctant to subject ourselves for a second time to the perils of the lethal A685 road. At the station it was cold and blustery, and as we alighted at Garsdale Head the rain started in earnest, blown on a boisterous west wind, and blotting out the hills.

The high route we had planned, following the ancient track over Thwaite Bridge and Mallerstang Commons seemed less than attractive in the conditions, and we opted for the minor B road which parallels the railway and climbs to the Mallerstang pass at Aisgill summit; on the heights above the pass the river Eden is born, and here are the Gates of Eden, where the infant river begins its descent into the valley on its way to the Solway Firth. We plodded on, watching the clouds swirling around the summit of Wild Boar Fell with the wind tugging at our waterproofs. On this wild and lonely road we met only one other walking couple and some struggling cyclists, but were surprised and overjoyed to find at Aisgill summit a smallholding offering coffee, accommodation and crafts.

The Sussex–born proprietor guessed what we were up to– 'You're not walking end–to–end are you?' and we spent three–quarters of an hour listening to his talk of the building of the railway, one of the epics of railway construction to be put alongside that of the Scottish West Coast route over Rannoch Moor. Despite its age (completed 1816) and alleged decrepitude we learned that the line had been used recently as a relief route for Intercity while the main west coast line was being electrified – and had survived the experience!

We were becoming tired with road–walking, and were glad to leave the road to pick up our route on the west bank of the river Eden, a small hill beck at this point. The path was ill-defined, just a line of rather ramshackle stiles, the occasional gate, and a farm where we were directed across a field redolent with recent muck–spreading. On the map it looked as though the route followed the river, but we soon found ourselves some fifty feet above it creeping cautiously round a placidly grazing bull, and finally had to claw our way up the hillside to avoid an impassable ravine above ruined Pendragon Castle. We extricated ourselves through a farmyard then found a good track to take us on a delightful green road round the flank of Birkett Common, the hillside covered with meadowsweet, marguerites and foxgloves.

We had found the afternoon's walk rather more sporting than the pleasant riverside stroll we had expected, and it was good to return to comfortable Fletcher House for a second night. The proprietor was busy attending to an American party just arriving who, we learned, were using Fletcher House as a base while doing the Coast–to–Coast, having transport to take them to start and finish of each day's stage. Talking to them later we heard that a rough time was had on Helvellyn, with, they said, sixty–mile–an–hour winds

We dined again at the Pennine Hotel and made various phone calls to arrange a rendezvous for Sunday, when Audrey would finish her part of the walk. Kirkby Stephen was full of bedraggled–looking backpackers searching for campsites and accommodation after what must have been a hard day in the conditions. After my experience of meeting so few in my travels I was surprised to discover this influx of people. It seemed as though the Coast–to–Coast walk had suddenly achieved the kind of popularity which the Pennine Way once had, possibly because of a recent televised repeat of the walk by Wainwright, not long before his death.

July 13th: With another short day ahead we lingered over breakfast next morning, being supplied with seconds of bacon, toast and home–made strawberry jam by a friendly assistant, who we suspected had noticed our habit of making sandwiches of any uneaten food for second breakfast on the way.

We had yet again to put on wet weather gear as we left. I'd searched in vain for a practicable off–road route to take us to our next objective, Appleby. The few rights of way shown on the map refused to join to form a continuous line, and I finally decided that we would have to go by minor roads. This was a pastoral landscape, dotted with small farms and patches of deciduous woodland, the whole forming a fertile corridor along the river Eden between the Pennines to the east and the Lake District fells to the west. The road climbed to follow a low ridge and we began to see to our right familiar shapes of the north Pennine hills emerging from the mists, the long ridge leading up to Cross Fell, the highest point of the Pennine way, with the pointed shapes of Dufton and Knock Pikes standing sentinel in front. It was an exciting moment to realise that we were so far north.

Going on, we soon heard the affronted bleating which we had come to recognise as associated with shearers, and turning a corner came upon the action in pens erected by the roadside. We joined an handful of interested spectators to watch the proceedings, which looked tremendously strenuous, hot and dirty. A team of three was working, one to retrieve each sheep in turn from those waiting in the pen, and to return it to the field where anxious offspring were waiting; one man did the actual shearing, working with electric shears operated from a portable generator, while the third handled the heavy fleeces, all working with impressive speed. It was hardly a warm day and I wondered if in this harsh northern climate the sheep missed their heavy coats.

In the early afternoon we climbed the steep hill past the Norman castle into Appleby, which used to be the county town of the old county of Westmorland before to the disgust of locals Westmorland was engulfed in the county of Cumbria. The town was *en fête* with a carnival going on by the river. We had time to spare, so visited the Copper Kettle for coffee and teacakes. One of the delights of the north country is that it is rare for a small town not to have a teashop, and we took full advantage of those we found.

We walked round the old town, and went to look at St. Lawrence's church, part twelfth century with bits added on later. Reading the history it came as a shock to discover that parts of the church had been destroyed in Border raids and to realise that I was less than fifty miles by road from Scotland. The end of the walk was approaching fast.

We had booked for the night at Kirkber farm, one and a half miles from Appleby, so walked up the steep hill under the viaduct carrying our old friend the Settle–Carlisle railway, and followed lanes under a new by–pass not marked on my outdated map. As happens so often on evening walks the sky had cleared and the declining sun was showing every fold of the Cross Fell range in green and gold detail, beautiful and inspiring. We came to the farm, a dark stone building crouched under the shadow of the hills, and met a welcoming Mrs Bell, who showed us to a room looking out on to the fells.

Our addresses for accommodation for the coming three nights were taken from a list compiled by the Cumbria Women's Institute, an excellent and economical way of publicising accommodation, both for users and suppliers, and we found our hostesses without exception friendly and hospitable. (Audrey's status as a bona fide paid–up member of her local Mother's Union assured her acceptance within the circle of women's organisations which include the Women's Institute.) We sat in the comfortable sitting–room watching the hills changing colour from gold to grey, drinking tea and eating home–made goodies, then watched Casualty, our favourite soap opera.

July 14th: I was beginning to feel desperately in need of a rest day after ten days of continuous walking and decided that come what may I must have a rest before tackling the stage over Cross Fell. The morning's walk to Dufton was only a short stroll , no more than five miles, but it felt an effort to take each step as if there were boulders in my rucksack. At Dufton we renewed acquaintance with the Pennine Way, which since we left it at Hawes had climbed lumpy Great Shunner Fell over to the enchanting Swale, had crossed Stainmoor to meet the river Tees at Middleton, and had traversed the wild and lonely country by Cauldron Snout and Maize Beck to descend into the Eden valley via spectacular High Cup.

I remembered how Rob and I had walked over the moors from Teesdale to Dufton on the day after a violent thunderstorm when small streams had become hazardous torrents. We had waded knee–deep in sodden vegetation to the Maize Beck crossing, and had arrived, magically, at the brink of High Cup as the mists rose like a curtain to reveal the Lake District fells in blue and gold.

We went into the Stag, an honest–to–goodness country pub full of locals talking about yesterday's carnival in Appleby. Two Pennine Way walkers came in, a father and son from Sheffield, descended from High Cup after a night camping above the Tees. Looking weather–beaten and travel–stained, they talked glowingly of their enjoyment of the walk, vowing that what they would really like to do would be to turn around at the end and walk back!

We waited around in Dufton for a while, sitting on a seat on the village green and half expecting John and Dick to appear. The pub closed, ejecting a number of people, mostly young men, seeming to have drunk more than was good for them, who got into their cars and drove away, I hoped not too far for the sake of other road–users. An older man approached me, walking rather unsteadily. He asked where was I walking back to...'not the Pennine Way...no...you're no longer a young woman.'

I'm sure he meant no harm and had I been feeling less tired I think I would have responded to his remark in a more friendly fashion, but I wasn't in the mood for discussion of my age, certainly not with someone who looked as if he had walked no further than the few hundred yards needed to get him to the pub for his Sunday drink; so I replied rather tartly, 'What's that got to do with anything?'. I'm not too sure what happened after that except that Audrey announced that 'My sister's walked from Beachy Head' to the small crowd now assembled. At some point my questioner must have retreated.

It was a short walk then to Knock and along the road to Slakes Farm, soon to be joined by John and Dick who had driven from Derby that morning. Another change was afoot; the four of us would spend the next two nights in the Eden valley, when Audrey and John would return to Derby, and Dick would join me for the final stages of the walk. The adventure seemed to be galloping along towards its end.

Interlude in Eden

Seeing Dick drive into the farm courtyard somehow put the whole enterprise into another gear; we had so often set out on walking trips together, from some starting point where we had left the car to be recovered later, that I felt as if a holiday was about to start. We ate a farmhouse meal supplemented with strawberries and wine from home and sat around a blazing fire swapping stories of exploits past and present. The four of us, Audrey, John, Dick and myself had much to talk about and plan for, and we had an animated discussion about the next part of the expedition. I was adamant that I needed a rest day; I had for a time run out of steam and wanted some space so that I could start again refreshed.

We saw Audrey and John off to Patterdale the next morning, where in conditions of sunshine and showers they did a walk to Boardale Hause. Dick drove the car to our next night's lodging at Kirkland, while I walked the four and a half miles from Slakes along winding lanes. This was pure pleasure; the clouds were low over dark Cross Fell but in the valley the sun shone, and in trainers and without a pack I felt light and unencumbered. The hedgerows were in full summer attire: meadow—sweet, cranesbill, foxgloves and columbines were in bloom and the scent of new—mown hay came from an adjoining field where a tractor was whirring. I realised that during the hundreds of miles of walking the stiffness had gone from my ankle and for the first time I was walking without intermittent pain.

The Eden valley is well named, spreading a green mantle over the miles that separate the Cross Fell massif and the Lakeland fells. The main roads, M6, A6, A66 which scar the countryside to the west and north seem to have made little impact on this corner of paradise north and east of Appleby, and the winding farm roads bear only local and holiday traffic, linking small villages, each no more than a farm and a smattering of houses.

Halfway to Kirkland Dick came jogging back to meet me; he had left the car at Kirkland House, opposite the church, where we were to spend the night.

Kirkland really is the end of the road; a quarter mile beyond the church tarmac turns into a stony track climbing high on to Cross Fell. This is a corpse road, used for many years for carrying coffins on foot over from Garrigill to the consecrated graveyard at Kirkland. Garrigill now deals with its own corpses, but the corpse road is a recognised route to Cross Fell, joining the Pennine Way a hundred metres below the mountain's summit.

We had coffee then drove to Langwathby station on the Settle–Carlisle line to reconnoitre a parking place for the car which we would leave to be recovered on our return from Scotland. Next stop Penrith, for some essential shopping.

Penrith, a busy gateway to the Lake District, nevertheless retains its character as an old market town, with fewer of the familiar multiple stores which sometimes make it difficult to know which English town you are in. We visited bookshop and supermarket, then drove back towards Kirkland watching showers and rainbows sweeping over Cross Fell. I was beginning to feel excited at the thought of climbing the corpse road tomorrow, my fatigue gone in the thought of the miles still to be covered and the knowledge that I was within reach of my objective, the Scottish borders.

Kirkland House was an imposing Victorian edifice built of the rose–coloured stone which adds warmth to the appearance of local buildings, and dating, we were to learn, from 1882, just two years older than our own house in Sydenham. One of only a half–dozen houses in this remote road–end, it had a wonderful feeling of peace and tranquillity. The furnishings, as in so many of the older houses where I was entertained, appeared not to have changed since the house was first occupied so seemed supremely appropriate to the setting adding to the sense of stability which permeated this whole area.

Audrey and John soon appeared, and we exclaimed at the size of our rooms, and the huge bathroom, big enough, Audrey said, to hold a party. Baths and hair–washing were the order of the day, then a look at Channel 4's report on the first days of the Tour de France, with Greg Lemond for a short time in the yellow jersey. We set out again in two cars,first to leave our Volkswagen at Langwathby station, then for the four of us to drive in the Timmins' Metro to the Stag in Milburn for a good pub meal, the congenial company adding to the enjoyment. The sky had cleared in the valley, and the setting sun was casting a lurid glow on the clouds still lowering on Cross Fell. We returned to watch a more favourable weather forecast, and to drink wine around a blazing fire.

I felt reluctant to leave idyllic Eden, but Scotland was just over the horizon. Next morning we separated, Audrey and John to drive back to Wharfedale where they climbed Buckden Pike in damp and muddy conditions, then drove to Lothersdale to stay at Burlington House. I marvelled that in an hour or two it was possible to drive the distance which had taken a week to cover on foot.

Dick and I turned away from the road, and headed for the hills.

9: A Small Town in a Faraway Country of which we know little

Tuesday July 16th: Before we had gone a quarter–mile we met a corporation sweeping the road; strange to see this manifestation of local authority in a little backwater where we hadn't seen a trace of litter. We followed the small beck for a while then left it to climb the shoulder of the hill, looking back from time to time to see showers sweeping over the Lakeland fells. The flowery verges disappeared, to be replaced by the coarse grasses of the open fellside, grazed by a few shorn sheep.

We were soon engulfed in cold dank mist, thankful for the unerring way in which the track led us on as we climbed steadily. The route twisted and turned through old mine workings, finally to emerge on open hillside and to renew acquaintance with the peat which I had last encountered back on Ickornshaw Moor. In the murk we strained to pick out one by one the line of cairns which now replaced the hard track; I was glad of Dick's comforting presence in this wild and hostile landscape.

A final huge cairn signalled the point where the Pennine Way descends from Cross Fell summit, at 2930 feet the highest point of the Pennine Way, to join the Corpse road; a few yards beyond it the shape of Greg's Hut loomed through the murk. This is an old miner's cottage now converted as an open bothy. Its two rooms contained only an old bed, a table and benches but this was welcome shelter in the conditions. We had a halt for second breakfast, thankful to have a roof over our heads. It was hard to believe that this was mid–July.

As we left the hut there was a sudden clearance of the kind that happens in the hills. The clouds parted and to the north we saw a long valley crossed by peat channels; in its depths a

Newcastleton

Kershope Bridge

Bewcastle

Scottish Border

Gilsland

Hadrian's Wall

Lambley

Knaresdale

Carlisle

Alston

Garrigill

△ Cross Fell

Kirkland

shining beck led down and down to where more than a thousand feet below, it joined the green valley of the South Tyne lit by weak shafts of sunlight. Beyond it rose more hills reaching into the far distance with hints of more to come. Behind us the whole ridge of mighty Cross Fell cleared momentarily, with the paraphernalia of the radar and weather station on Great Dun Fell standing out like some futuristic furnishings from a science fiction story.

As fast as they had dispersed the clouds closed in again; we rooted around the disused mine workings to find pieces of blue crystalline fluorspar, then as the rain started in earnest began the descent to Garrigill, eight miles of unrelenting downhill trudge. The weather forecast had been for a brighter afternoon, but obviously this wasn't going to apply to the North Pennines; the showers became more frequent and the cold west wind battered us unremittingly, so we were glad to reach the quiet village street at Garrigill.

Around the corner from where the Corpse road enters the village there used to be a teashop, just the front room of an ordinary cottage, run by two old ladies, and a truly welcome sight for survivors of Cross Fell. In 1978 we had paid just twenty pence each for a huge pot of tea and plates of scones. I was disappointed to see that the teashop was no longer there, only a flat row of shuttered cottages with nothing to show where hundreds of thirsty walkers must have rested.

We went to look in the church, another refuge for benighted travellers, who are permitted to use it for overnight bivouacs if all else fails. Next stop was the post office, where we had booked, a tiny place in sharp contrast to the noble proportions of Kirkland House, but with lots of hot bathwater, and the usual welcoming tea. We looked at a better weather forecast, caught up on the Tour de France, and went next door to the George and Dragon; outside were three huge packs, their owners Pennine Wayfarers from Sheffield, doing the walk the hard way with camping gear. We ate fish and chips by a splendid fire and strolled around the village green in the last of the evening light. This was the last day of week 8, leaving me forty miles from Newcastleton.

July 17th: We left Garrigill in sunshine, encountering a small flurry of walkers which we soon put behind us, to join the South Tyne river, burbling along through green meadows in startling contrast to bleak Cross Fell. Before long we were in Alston just in time for morning coffee. We left the river to climb on to the open moor; the scenery here is not spectacular but has a wonderful sense of space, sparsely populated with widely separated stone dwellings and having that special light which seems to infuse the northern counties; the rolling moors with the horizon constantly changing beckon the traveller on to limitless far distances.

We passed the Roman fort of Whitley Castle, set high on a strategic point overlooking the valley, climbed many stone walls by beautifully carpentered step stiles, crossed a road and came to the river again, grown larger now, flowing through a gorge and into a steep–sided wooded valley. At Slaggyford we abandoned the footsteps of the Romans on Maiden Way for the disused railtrack, surely an alternative Pennine Way judging by the numbers of bootmarks. The flowers that I associated with the north country of my youth were growing in abundance: yarrow, the vetches, comfrey, borage and knapweed. Wagtails foraged busily for insects almost under our feet. Somewhere along this section we had our first glimpse of the Whin Sill, the line of dolerite crags which mark the course of Hadrian's Wall, where we would leave the Pennine Way.

We climbed an embankment, crossed two fields, and went down a little loop road to find Stonehall, another old farmhouse where we spent the night, returning to the rail track next morning. The fine weather was bringing out the flies for which this section of the Pennine Way is notorious. Hamish Brown writes of nightmarish hordes of flies making life miserable for himself and companion Border collie Storm on these hills. A hat helps in repelling these nuisances, and I realised that I had forgotten to bring with me the old friendly one which has accompanied me on many Scottish expeditions.

We soon came to the station house, where progress along the railtrack was barred by private land. Here there was a splendid view down to the South Tyne, now a sizeable water-course, spanned by the Lambley viaduct, a marvel of Victorian engineering. I read later that British Rail is attempting to sell off this and many other relics of the heyday of railway travel, unwilling to meet the costs of safe maintenance; I hope that there will be organisations willing and able to preserve these magnificent monuments to a past century.

We found our way to the road, at the corner where the A689 turns west to head for Brampton and Carlisle. In a few yards we rejoined the Pennine Way as it descended from Hartleybury Common, and set off in worsening weather. The way led on to what was truly a blasted heath, abandoned industrial land, with the end of an old mineral railway almost hidden under growing vegetation. We passed by a crumbling ruined farmhouse, and went on along rudimentary paths which soon disappeared in sour and neglected moorland.

We picked our way carefully across this trackless waste, did some intricate navigation to take us across the green valley of the Hartleyburn, and climbed over squelchingly wet tussocky ground to reach the trig point marking the summit of the second Black Hill of the Pennine Way. (I had chickened out of attempting the first one in Cheshire).

This was better; the Whin Sill appeared off to our right, much closer now, frozen waves of rock rippling away into the distance. Across our front was a green valley, marking the Tyne Gap, the narrowest piece of Britain, linking the Solway Firth to the west with Tynemouth to the east. Like other coast–to–coast corridors, the Tyne Gap is a transport highway for road and rail, as well as the place chosen by Emperor Hadrian to site the Roman Wall, designed to separate the Romans from the northern barbarians. The South Tyne had turned away to the east on its way to the sea through industrial Tyneside. We found a dry spot on this wet summit to eat our lunch and enjoy some brief sunshine.

We descended more wet moorland to Gap Shield where we bade a final farewell to the Pennine Way, which from here would head for Hadrian's Wall to follow it almost to the Roman fort at Housestead's, then cross the Wark and Redesdale Forests to the final obstacle of the Cheviot Hills. I had decided to take the more direct route to Scotland. I had enjoyed my second encounter with the Pennine Way, but rather shared Wainwright's conclusion: 'You won't come across me anywhere along the Pennine Way. I've had enough of it'. As we left the Pennine Way my six hundredth mile was completed

We dodged the roaring traffic of the A69 trunk road, and set off down the lane opposite, an undulating road passing uneven green fields grazed by pale cattle, relatives of the French Charollais. Signs of Roman occupation were everywhere, directions to Roman camps and fortifications. Down a hill we came into our destination, Gilsland, set in a steep–sided valley, a few houses, a pub, shop, and station.

The bridge spanning the Irthing river marks a county boundary, so we walked from Northumbria into Cumbria to find Howard House Farm, set high on the hillside.This was another address from Cumbria Women's Institute, but also one of a consortium of farms offering welcome accommodation in a sparsely populated area. Mrs Woodmass had accumulated a fund of information about the district which we were able to use in planning our route from here.

We learned that the Tornado bombers which had been screeching over us for most of the day were engaged in an exercise deferred from the Gulf War, and that the Danger Area signs with which our OS map was studded related to the bombing range at Spadeadam Farm in the unpopulated country to the north. I was surprised that people seemed to accept the intrusive presence of the fighter aircraft so philosophically; I would find it an irritation both from noise pollution and from restricted access to the countryside.

At Howard House the talk was of the bad summer, and how it had as yet been impossible to cut the hay. I thought of the South Downs, where eight weeks ago the hay harvest had been in full swing.

July 19th: The bridleway marked Roman Road which we had hoped to use on our next stage had been closed, so we devised a plan B to avoid the risk of being targets of dive–bombers. We took the B road westward out of Gilsland, leaving it to descend steeply on a footpath into a wooded valley; an equally steep ascent brought us out at a right–angled bend in a narrow lane.

We looked south from this high point across the green valley with lorries looking like Dinky toys streaking along the main road, and beyond it to the dark moors we had crossed yesterday. Immediately across the road from us was Hadrian's Wall.

It might be any well–made old wall, here just bordering a country road, old dark stones, with gaps like missing teeth so it comes as a shock to realise that these stones and mortar were assembled nearly two thousand years ago.

The Berlin Wall was just that, a wall, with look–out points along its length. Hadrian's Wall was a huge defensive complex, with strong points at regular intervals, and an infrastructure of large forts, each having a separate regiment allotted to it. An enormous garrison of fifteen to sixteen thousand men was stationed on the wall. These troops were not all Romans, but came from all corners of the Roman Empire, and researches have shown that the soldiers often married local women; their sons in turn followed their fathers' profession, so the occupying force went through a process of being assimilated into British society.

Three Roman legions were stationed in Britain in Hadrian's day, at Caerleon–on–Usk on the Welsh Border, at Chester, and at York. Detachments from all three legions did the main body of work in the five years it took to build the main structure. The builders then returned to the greater comfort of their fortresses, leaving the defence of the Wall to auxiliary troops.

I can't imagine anyone seeing Hadrian's Wall for the first time and not being enthralled by its feeling of history, and by the realisation that the Romans were able to bring aspects of their advanced civilisation into a hostile environment in harsh and unyielding terrain. Mrs Woodmass had said that Bewcastle, where we were headed, was 'like the end of the earth'. How much more so must it have seemed to these young men, so far from home?

Much of the Wall has been destroyed, its stones removed for other building, but excavation continues on remaining sections. We walked for a quarter–mile to reach Birdoswald, where granaries have been unearthed in a fine state of preservation, massively built, with huge wooden beams. We went in the newly opened visitor centre, to inspect some of the finds: a polished metal helmet looking as if discarded yesterday by its owner; various coins and weapons; and pieces of wall inscribed with the names of its builders.

We went on along the line of the wall for a while, eventually leaving it to follow a meandering farm road back to the B6318, which we crossed. The B6318 would weave a tortuous thread of a route ultimately to arrive in Newcastleton; we hoped to achieve the same destination more directly.

The Tornadoes seemed to have been grounded for the weekend, and all was peace as we followed first tarmac then a farm track north. We passed a farm where we were glad that a stout gate separated us from some enthusiastic guard dogs, and crossed a stream where we surprised a grey heron fishing. A field footpath led us to an unfenced mountain road climbing a ridge; we sat on a grassy hillside to eat lunch and looked across a fertile landscape to see the Solway Firth shining in the distance, my first view of the sea since the Cotswolds.

We came eventually to Bewcastle, hardly recognisable as a village. The pub, one of just a half–dozen buildings, was firmly shut, and no one was about. We crossed the road bridge over the river, the Kirk Beck, and turned on to a footpath over the hillside. This took us past yet another Roman fort, the most northerly outpost of Hadrian's Wall, as part of its protective fortifications. We climbed a hill across a meadow knee–deep in grass, poppies and marguerites, and regained the unfenced road a few yards from Park School House. The house is long disused as a school, but can never have had a large number of pupils in this sparsely populated area.

Mrs Gee was waiting for us at the gate and produced scones and cake to go with our afternoon tea. We learned that this is a retired couple, the husband an ex–schoolmaster, moved to this remote area from the Midlands some years ago. Mr Gee is an expert on clocks, and the bungalow was full of his work, clocks in all stages of construction.

The walk was fast drawing to its close. Just a few miles up the road was Scotland and tomorrow I would be on my way home. Like all endings, this one seemed to be coming too quickly. One part of me was ready for calling a halt; I was beginning to feel the need of a breathing space, to assimilate my experiences and to make sense of them. I had felt myself running out of curiosity because of the sheer volume of sensations and sights. The other part wanted to go on, was reluctant to return to face all the minutiae of everyday life which I knew were waiting for me. I reassured myself that over the border Scotland was waiting and would still be there next year; the best was yet to be.

Walking through the borders is truly a walk through history, fierce and terrible. Every foot of this beautiful region has been at some time bloodily fought over. The relative success of the Romans in defending the border against the Pictish hordes was succeeded after their departure in the fourth century by more centuries of turmoil, only to be resolved by an Act of Union. The line of the border had to be hammered out almost foot by painful foot along the natural boundaries, the rivers Tweed and Esk, and the mountain barrier of the Cheviot Hills.

It's odd, isn't it, that the Borders are called Scottish, since northern England is equally border country?

Mr Gee told us that Bewcastle is said to mark the furthest point north penetrated by the Normans after the invasion of 1066; they built a castle there against fierce and persistent opposition from the Scottish defenders. Indeed Rey Cross on the Pass of Stainmore nearly fifty miles to the south is said to have marked the English–Scottish border at the time of William the Conqueror, so the English in later centuries were less successful than the Romans, who were able to reach and build the Antonine Wall across the Forth–Clyde gap, which I was to cross when I was over a hundred miles closer to Cape Wrath. The opposition of the time was thereby confined to the Highland regions.

July 20th: The little road we took to the border is scarcely more than a farm track for the first few miles, with grass growing in the middle, gates to open and cattle–grids to cross. There was a profusion of flowers surpassing any I had seen so far on the journey; the verges were carpeted with an array of low–growing plants, vetches, ragged robin, knapweed, harebells which are the real bluebells of Scotland, and spotted orchis, against a backdrop of tall Scottish thistles, foxgloves, amd the purple of the willow–herb, a plant we had always associated with Scotland, where its vibrant colour makes the fireweed seen in southern counties seem a poor relation. Hidden amongst this wealth we found a butterfly orchid. For the first hour not a car came by.

We climbed a hill and entered deep pine forest, row upon row of dark trees, outposts of countless acres of country to the north and east planted by the Forestry Commission. It began to rain gently and determinedly. In a lull we came into a clearing and found a log to sit on to eat second breakfast, soon to be discovered by midges, outliers of the Scottish hordes beyond the border come to greet us. These unwelcome reminders of a Scottish plague made me feel better about cutting the walk short at this point; midges tend to increase in ferocity with the advance of summer and I hoped to be next in Scotland come June before the plague became unmanageable.

The small dwelling marked 'inn' on the map turned out to be between owners, peopled only by workmen and a noisy dog. Another mile, and we came to the top of a hill; a bird of prey soared out of the forest; and we looked across into Scotland.

Below us a small bridge spanned a river; at its near bank the forest ended abruptly, and beyond rose smooth green hills with a narrow white road winding away on the further side. This was the Kershope Burn, marking one of the most hotly disputed parts of the border, Mr Gee had said. At one time it had been a place for marriages between eloping couples from England.

Far to our left was a broad valley, flanked by higher rougher hills. It sounds crazy to say it, but it looked like an approaching frontier, and I felt really excited to see this abrupt change in the scenery. It just wouldn't have seemed right to have had no visible sign of this significant boundary.

I started to walk down the winding hill, with Dick staying behind to take photographs. The scene is imprinted on my memory as if engraved there: the wide unpeopled view, the wide sky, the green hills ahead, and the dark forest we were leaving behind.

The heavens opened as I was setting foot on the bridge, real honest–to–goodness rain, none of your Scotch mist. With no shelter, I stood on the bridge to be photographed, one foot in England and one in Scotland, face scarcely visible under Goretex hood. I looked for a frontier post or a border guard, but there was nothing, only a sign saying that this was the Kershope Forest and a warning notice exhorting motorists to look out for straying sheep.

We plodded on along the road for the two and a half miles towards Newcastleton. After a while the rain stopped and we came to the Liddel Water, and walked by it into town. A long Scottish town, its main street flanked by tall grey houses, a square with trees and two hotels. I needed to say to someone 'I've just walked from Beachy Head', but no one looked at all curious, so I went into the telephone box and called Audrey in Derby to give her the news. We looked at bus timetables and found that we had an hour and a half to wait for the bus to Carlisle.

The black cloud which had taken up station over Newcastleton started to discharge its contents again; we looked around for shelter, discovered that the pubs were just closing, so hurried up the street to find a small teashop. We ordered coffee and toasted teacakes, lingered as long as we could in disposing of them, then, displaced by the numbers of other customers also escaping from the weather, wandered back into the square, where it was still raining relentlessly. There was not even a bus shelter to give any cover, and for a time we huddled under some trees until the rain started cascading down our necks.

In desperation I suggested we visit the craft fair which I had seen advertised. This was round the corner in the village hall. There was a sizeable vestibule where we took off and hung up dripping cagoules, then paid twenty pence admission fee.

I have to say that it wasn't much of a craft fair in the way I'd imagined it; no hand–thrown pottery, no paintings by local artists, and no trendy hand–knitted sweaters. Instead there were stalls selling second–hand books and children's clothes and bric–a–brac. Our presence, however, made something of an impact, travel–stained and weather–beaten as we were among the neat twin–sets and skirts. There could have been no more effective way to spread the news of my exploit; I could almost hear the words 'she's walked from Beachy Head' being passed from person to person like an impromptu game of Chinese Whispers.

Embarrassed by the sudden notoriety we escaped into the vestibule where there were thoughtfully provided seats. People came to talk to us, and there we waited until it was time to cross the road, still in pouring rain, to the bus stop.

There isn't much more to tell. The bus came, and as we drove into England the sun came out; it had been shining all day in Carlisle, said the driver. Twenty–four hours later I was walking into my study at home, looking just as I had left it. It seemed odd to realise that I had missed a whole chunk of the summer. Somewhere there was a feeling that the world should have stopped for me while I escaped into another dimension like a time–traveller. I couldn't quite believe that I had been away.

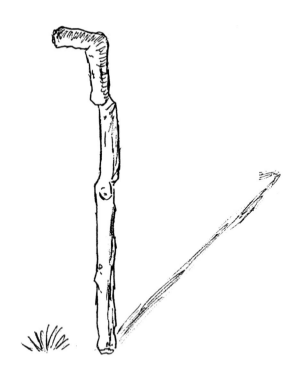

PART 2: SCOTLAND

10: The end is where we start from.

When you set out for Ithaka
Pray that the road is long
Full of adventure and discoveries
But do not hurry the journey...

Cavafy

It was three hundred and thirty–nine miles from our house in Sydenham to the Kershope Bridge on the Scottish border, not much more than half the number of miles I had walked the previous year from Beachy Head

The months following my return from Newcastleton had flown by. I have always found myself wanting to do two things at once, and along with the lengthy planning for my end–to–end walk I had been studying for a Master's degree, a long–held ambition for which my retirement in 1988 had provided the opportunity. Now it was crunch time; I had a dissertation to write, and this was to occupy the whole summer, along with catching up with friends and family.

Before, it seemed, I could turn round, it was Christmas. I was trying hard to get fit enough to do the London Marathon postponed from last year; we were welcoming Rob home from a world tour, and we were looking forward (if that's an appropriate way to put it) to a General Election. There seemed little enough time to prepare for walking through Scotland.

Saturday May 16th: Against all expectations, however, I was back here on a hot May afternoon at this beautiful spot, so familiar even after only one previous visit. I had driven with

Edinburgh

East Calder

Pentland Hills

Cauldstone Slap

West Linton

Lyne

Peebles

TWEEDDALE

Traquair

Minchmuir

Selkirk

HILLS

TEVIOT

Hawick

Whitrope Tunnel

Newcastleton

Kershope Bridge

Dick from the over–populated southern counties along the busy main roads with the traffic, the noise and the numbers of people steadily decreasing as we drove north. With the sun beating down, we left the main road at Hadrian's Wall, and drove along twisting lanes to recover the route along which we had walked last July. I became increasingly excited as we began to recognise familiar features: the place where we had stopped to put on waterproofs; where we had been attacked by midges at second breakfast; the inn, still with closed doors, which was being refurbished last year. Minutes later we were descending the winding road to the bridge where I had huddled in a waterproof to have my picture taken.

We pulled into a parking spot on the English side and made tea; the sun shone brilliantly from an unpolluted sky, the little river burbled contentedly beside us, the only sound to be heard, as if the world of noise and cars and hurry had ceased to exist. We took photographs and I took the first steps into Scotland, to walk the two and a half miles into Newcastleton.

I suppose that after last year's exploit I should have thought of myself as an experienced end–to–ender, but it didn't seem like that at all, although I knew myself to be fitter than last year. I was aware that walking through Scotland would impose more demands than through England. The terrain would be rougher and sometimes pathless, there would be longer stretches between places where I could stay, and there would be hazards in the way of rivers to cross and wilderness to negotiate. I think I had no firm expectation of completing the walk, and had thus made an unconscious decision that I wouldn't think about it too much, but would tackle each problem as I came to it.

When therefore people asked me, as they often did, about how, once there, I would get back from Cape Wrath, I avoided replying, since I couldn't actually see myself getting there at all. For the moment I was more concerned with how I would reach tomorrow's target destination, Hawick. I was beginning to see the walk as a huge jigsaw with a few pieces missing, which I hoped to fit into place as I went along. It did, however, feel wonderful to be out on the trail once more as, leaving my rucksack in the car for Dick to take to Newcastleton, I set off from Kershope

Bridge feeling full of energy and renewed enthusiasm.

Almost immediately the feeling came back, of having a limitless road before me, of being freed from all the trappings of daily existence; just as on Beachy Head, the glass screen came down between me and the outside world, which could be forgotten for a while. All that I had to do was to concentrate on those actions and activities which would bring me to Cape Wrath and everything else was subordinate to that one aim.

I took in every detail along the quiet road: the clarity of the hills under cloudless skies, the gentle gurgle of the accompanying stream, and the wealth of spring flowers in the verges, primroses, celandine, geum, ladysmock, wild garlic, some marsh marigolds in the ditch, wood anemones and drifts of bluebells under the trees. A cuckoo called, and I came into Newcastleton watching flights of mallards above the river.

'It doesn't seem right that it isn't raining,' said Dick coming out to meet me. We walked into the square, which had the appearance of a French town, with its tall flat-fronted houses. There had been a wedding, and people in their finery were sitting outside the hotel drinking and laughing. We booked into the Grapes Hotel, a year late.

After dinner we walked around the now quiet town, with the sun not yet set at this northern latitude, and it warm enough in mid-May not to need a coat. We found the site of Newcastleton old railway station and the start of the disused line which I was hoping to use for to-morrow's walk, and made a plan, for Dick to provide transport back-up before setting off on the drive back to London.

May 17th. On another cloudless morning I set off along the rail track, soft underfoot, carpeted with primroses and violets. I came out on an embankment and descended to meet the minor road for a three-mile road walk to Hermitage. Dick met me here, having carried out some research into whether the track was passable.

This was the Waverley line, which used to run from Edinburgh to Carlisle before being closed against public opposition in 1969. Dick had discovered from the occupier of a cottage along the road that the track could be walked for most of the way from Newcastleton to Hawick, including the mile-long Whitrope tunnel at the summit of the railway, over a thousand feet above sea level. The idea of walking through a disused tunnel sounded interesting, and Dick decided to come with me, which seemed a good idea. I wasn't sure what we would find there.

We reached the high point, Dick by car and I on foot; the man from the cottage came out to talk, and to direct us up a high embankment to the tunnel entrance, black and forbidding in the bright sunshine. 'If you don't come back for the car I'll send out a search party,' he said; which didn't really boost my confidence. We had gone no more than a hundred yards when my small torch gave out and we had to rely on the faint gleam from Dick's; we had not bargained for a walk in the dark.

After the outside torrid midday heat, I shivered in the gloom. The ground was covered in boulders, and we felt our way along holding on to the damp walls of the tunnel; it was like being in an underground cavern. There was a sound of water falling and we wondered if we would come across an impassable stream, but we soon discovered that water was seeping through the roof; we ran the gauntlet of the heavy warm shower, like being under an automatic sprinkler.

A pinhole of light appeared ahead; we couldn't quite believe that this was the tunnel's exit, it seemed so minute, but with every step the light intensified. Soon we were able to see where we were putting our feet, and after what seemed longer than the twenty minutes it had taken we were stepping out into the sunshine. On the track a few feet away a roe deer was grazing. It saw us only seconds before we reached it, and scampered off into the undergrowth.

We continued between low forested hills, the track aiming directly for Hawick in the way only railways can; we had moved away from the road, and it seemed impossibly peaceful, all memories of the preoccupations and bustle of preparation fading effortlessly. We came to a place where the track was interrupted by a farm road, and scrambled up an embankment on its far side to reach a high viaduct. Dick left me to jog back to the car, and I talked to a couple who asked how far I had walked and where I was going. What was I to say? I settled for saying I'd walked from the border and left it at that. I think I was feeling that I needed to get some distance under my boots before I could say I'd walked from Beachy Head.

The track began its gradual descent, and the countryside changed from bare moorland to cultivated fields with sheep grazing. Rounded green hills topped by trees bordered the wayside and obstacles like gates and fences became more frequent. Eventually the track dived through soggy undergrowth beneath a decrepit–looking bridge and came up against a mass of brambles and thickly growing vegetation; it looked, and was, impenetrable. Enough was enough; I climbed an embankment and crossed a field to reach a minor road at the summit of a steep hill. There was activity here, some sort of a car rally in progress, with the noise of revving engines making a contrast to the previous Sunday peace.

I descended the hill to where the Hawick road crossed a bridge; Dick had parked the car and was waiting with tea. It was the moment of truth, when lightweight trainers were discarded for business–like boots. We parted, Dick to drive the four miles to Hawick where he would leave my rucksack at the house where I had booked bed and breakfast, then would start the long drive home. It felt as if this was where the walk really began for me; for the next two hundred miles or so I was on my own.

The day was wearing into evening as I set off along the road, now busy with motorists returning from the rally, but the small spate of traffic quickly died away. Four miles seems a long way at the end of a twenty–mile day, but I soon fell into a reverie thinking my own thoughts and secure in the knowledge that bath and bed were not too far away.

The road wound along the valley following the course of the river, and came to a place where it turned sharply to cross a bridge. Across the road were some farm buildings and a yard where some people were standing by a fire cooking something. The acrid scent of woodsmoke rose in the evening air, together with the sound of good strong Scottish voices singing:

'a sweeter song has cheered me
at the evening's gentle close
and I've seen an eye still brighter
than the dewdrop on the rose'

The sound followed me along the road and I thought how well it suited the whole scene, and what a fine introduction to Scotland. The walk was coming to life from its tentative beginnings, and I looked eagerly ahead to the new places I would see and people I would meet as I came into the outskirts of Hawick, walked through the town, and crossed the river Teviot to find my lodging in a quiet side road.

I drank tea with my hostess Mrs Herbert and her mother and we talked about the Waverley line railway. I discovered that Mrs Herbert's father had been a relief signalman and the family had lived at Riccarton Junction when the line was still in operation. This was the junction deep in Newcastleton Forest where lines diverged to Carlisle and Hexham; Riccarton had once housed a thriving community. There was no motor road to the junction, so the railway was used for all transport, to school, to church, and for all goods and services. With the closing of the railway, the community ceased to be viable, and was now derelict.

I was to find that many people I talked to had a fund of knowledge about the railway, which was visited by railway enthusiasts as well as people like myself using it for a direct walker's route. People talked nostalgically about the impact on communities of the decline of railways, and this was clear to see, in the many abandoned dwellings along the route of the Waverley line.

I soaked my weary sunburned limbs in one of the outsize baths typically to be found in older Scottish dwellings, sank gratefully into an equally large bed, and fell asleep watching Mastermind. *May 18th:* I walked through streets of sturdy stone-built houses, under more cloudless skies. Passers-by exchanged greetings: 'It's a braw day'. I had arrived in Scotland just a day after the end of some unprecedentedly wet spring weather, and everyone looked pleased to be alive. The suburban road turned into a country lane, climbing high above the town, then becoming a rough farm track.

Border country can be wild and lonely as in the Cheviot Hills or dark and forbidding in the depths of the pine forests. Here it was open and friendly, the land ablaze with the bonnie broom, the real spring emblem of Scotland, its colour surely like no other yellow in the world. Ahead green hills rolled away to the horizon, beckoning invitingly to the Southern Uplands I was aiming to cross the next day. The farmer came along driving a buggy and stopped to talk. Where was I making for he asked. I replied Selkirk, my night's stop. And after that? I was making for the West Highland Way, I said. And after that? I realised that the game was up and confessed I was bound for Cape Wrath. There was a sense of release in saying it. He said, 'I thought it was something like that,' and, fervently, 'you lucky thing'. He told me how he had moved to the Borders only the previous year from Yorkshire, and spoke lovingly of the land he had adopted as his own.

I'd been neglecting to follow my route on the map, and in another mile found myself high on a hill, the track leading into the yard of a disused farm and disappearing. I reproached myself for not taking more heed of my surroundings and retraced my steps, giving myself an extra mile to walk, and finding that with the weight of a pack I was getting twinges from the backache which had plagued me all last year. I found my track, an old drove road leading through fields dotted with sheep to reach the main A7 road and continued along more lanes, making for a place with the endearing name of Dimpleknowe, where my map said there was a ford across the Ale Water.

Just to check, I called in at a cottage at the top of the hill to find out if there was a footbridge, the kind of crossing I was accustomed to finding over fords in Surrey and Kent. The young woman I spoke to said oh yes, she thought there was a bridge, but after descending the steep hill to the farm and finding my way through a securely fastened gate and a muddy farmyard I found only a fast-flowing stream with the track emerging on its far bank. There were signs that there had once been a bridge in some rotted timbers but any trace even of a ford had vanished.

Had I been in Northern Scotland I'm sure I wouldn't have thought twice about removing socks and wading across, but I wasn't psychologically prepared to take such drastic action in the civilised Borders. I retreated, toiled up the hill in the glare of the afternoon sun, and made for the road bridge a mile or so away, realising I was adding three miles to what I had expected to be an easy day. I sat by the roadside to eat my lunch sandwich,

126

discovering that the reason the time, five to two, which my watch was registering seemed rather early was that the watch had stopped and needed a new battery.

I decided I wasn't enjoying today. It was too hot and I was feeling the effect of yesterday's exertions. Walking on tarmac makes few demands in terms of route–finding or difficulty of terrain but the very ease creates its own tedium. I found myself counting the miles in a way I would not have done in more demanding country. It was a relief to reach the main road about a mile from Selkirk.

I called in at the petrol filling station to ask directions to my B&B, and the friendly attendant drew me a map. I was glad it was only just up the road; it had been another nine–hour day and I was sunburned, hungry and dehydrated. I drank pints of tea and ate the remnants of my provisions for an evening meal, too weary to go out to look for food. Still and all, I discovered I had crossed one map from south to north, and the view from my window was of the Minchmuir hills on the Southern Upland Way, where I would be tomorrow.

May 19th: I walked through the town, to cross the Ettrick Water not far from where it flows into the Tweed, that greatest of Border rivers. At Philiphaugh Farm I left the tarmac to climb uphill through pinewoods and out on to open hillside, following a path which led me to where a gate opened on to a crossing of tracks on a ridge–top. This was familiar country, where I had walked with Dick four years ago, and I would follow it to Traquair where I was to spend the night.

Besides being a section of a long–distance trail, the Minchmuir is an ancient track known to have been in use as far back as the 13th century and used since then as a highway and drove road. Now it is well frequented by those walking the two hundred miles or so across Scotland from Portpatrick to Cocksburnpath. I was soon to meet people as I climbed the rise to the prominent cairns of the Three Brethren, which mark estate boundaries. Last time I had been here was in thick mist, but today there was ample opportunity to stop and look at the view across the Tweed valley, with the familiar shape of the Eildon Hills beyond.

After yesterday's heat and tarmac it was good to be out on the hill and see the track winding ahead. After a spate of walkers in a led party, the foot traffic died away and there was time to relish the views, with increasing haze blanketing the far distance as the day wore on. I followed the track as it wound around a grassy hillside and on to the heather slopes of the high point Broome Law, then descended as it led into regimented forestry land.

I turned a corner to find a family group picnicking by a bank of daffodils, of all things, just below the place where the spring known as the Cheese Well emerges from the hillside, cheese because of the gifts of food which travellers were wont to leave to appease the fairies. I stopped to sample the water, cool and refreshing. This was another meeting place; three laden back-packers toiled up the hill from below, to drink thirstily.

From there it was downhill all the way to reach the road at Traquair, a long descent hard on the back and feet but the way carpeted with all the spring flowers and the occasional surprise like a clump of yellow Welsh poppies. A hare came lolloping along the track, spied me, stood stock still, then turned tail. I came out of the forest on to a steep stony lane through farmland dotted with the white Charollais cattle which seem to be the preferred breed of the Borders.

From the road it was just a step to the drive of Traquair Bank, a handsome farmhouse on the estate of ancient Traquair House, overlooking the valley of the Tweed with a view across to the town of Innerleithen. Traquair House claims to be the oldest inhabited house in Scotland, and has all sorts of interesting features including its own brewery, but you have to be there at the right time; the house was not open to visitors just now.

My fellow guests were two lively women farmers from Derry in Ulster and a Lancashire couple, friendly and talkative. Dinner was a sociable meal, with talk of travel, families, and the troubles in Ulster. This was the first time, I realised, that I had heard Ulster people talking about the troubles; some kind of union with the south they thought was eventually inevitable. Mrs Caird, our hostess, came in to talk; the Ulsterwomen, farmers themselves, knew just the right questions to ask, ones that townspeople like myself would never think of, and I listened in fascination, to talk about the awful spring weather when lambs had died from hypothermia, about the price of lambs in the market, and the kind of breeding bulls used, all the common everyday talk of the farming community.

May 20th: Morale at a low ebb; what, I kept asking myself, am I doing here? I'd hoped there might be a way along the river but was forced on to the road, a nice enough one through green countryside, past grazing cattle, horses, pheasants and rookeries, with the full swiftly flowing Tweed as a companion, but my back hurt, enough so there was nothing to take my mind off it. I was glad to arrive in Peebles in the early afternoon and to sit for a while on the green banks of the river looking at the view of the handsome town. I went and found a policeman to ask him the way to Dukehaugh where I was staying and he called up the station on his radio to find out!

I had planned two short days as a semi-rest period, so left my rucksack and went into town, visited the Tourist Information Centre, a great and helpful resource for End-to-Enders, and had high tea. I spent the evening with my landlady Mrs Kampmann and her African grey parrot called Aku, at least that's what it sounded like, I think from the Swahili for parrot. Aku was very talkative, keeping up a constant stream of chatter and singing for us 'Oh dear what can the matter be' and 'Polly put the kettle on' – his two party pieces. Aku was finally silenced by putting a blanket on his cage, the equivalent, I imagine, of putting the dormouse in the teapot.

I nearly fell asleep again watching the Chelsea Flower Show. At the same time last year I was on the South Downs Way, I remembered.

May 21st: The news was of torrential rain in Glasgow, and a much cooler day with grey skies. I went into town to pick up mail, maps and a replacement watch, and made another visit to Tourist Information to book future nights' accommodation, fitting more bits of the jigsaw into place. I took an extended coffee break in the local cafe to sort out literature and pack a parcel to send home, then back to pick up my pack and away by early afternoon.

My route, on the waymarked Tweed Valley Walk, led along the

tailored banks of the river Tweed, parkland and large old trees, soft grass underfoot, then into woods; a group of canoeists came swooping around the curve of a wide bend. I passed below Neidpath Castle standing high on the hillside and climbed on to the railway viaduct which crosses the river. It was cool enough to wear jersey and cagoule with clouds down on the surrounding hills and a hint of moisture in the air, but I had recovered from yesterday's fatigue and enjoyed the easy walk. I came to Lyne station where the path turns for home, crossed the main road, and climbed a hill to Lyne Farm, on the lower slopes of the Meldon Hills.

Lyne Farm was a family–run place, with two small children, Zara and Callum, both eager to show me around, so after I had eaten a vast meal we looked at the new foal, Moonlight, tadpoles in a pond, and pet lambs who came to be fed. Like Mrs Caird at Traquair, Mrs Waddell's passion was for raising and showing horses, and there were many trophies on display recording successes at shows. There was talk again of how disastrous the lambing season had been, with dozens of new–born lambs unable to survive the bitterly cold sleet of the early spring.

Looking at progress I found that I had walked across a second map despite feeling I had been going at a snail's pace, and was on target for my next objective, the Forth and Clyde Canal.

May 22nd: I followed the Lyne river all next day to West Lynton, through beautiful rolling countryside. A brisk east wind was blowing and through the heat haze there were enticing views ahead of the Pentland Hills I should be crossing tomorrow. Beyond were the canals I was making for.

Medwyn House was full for the weekend, but I was offered the self–catering flat; this felt a bit lonely, but I was intrigued to learn that Ron Scholes had stayed here. Mrs Waterston told me that this was the place where end–to–enders often felt at a low ebb, my feelings exactly. I remembered that this was the English Spring Holiday weekend; last year at the same time I had been on the verge of giving up.

I looked at Ron Scholes' book, *Understanding the Countryside* [Moorland 1985], an extremely professional piece of work and packed with information.

May 23rd: It was a grey morning, with mist down to the road as I set off, wearing thermal gear under my shirt and soon adding Goretex, hat and gloves. Medwyn House gave a good start to the day, being on the route of a great drove road which crosses Cauldstane Slap. This started on tarmac along a single-track unfenced road to reach Baddinsgill Farm and reservoir, becoming a Land Rover Track and finally a footpath through the heather. I was soon in cold cloud which didn't look like dispersing.

A walker overtook me, another end-to-ender I soon discovered. He was seven weeks into the walk from Land's End, and was following the John Hillaby route through Stirling. I've already done the West Highland Way,' he said, and I wondered if that meant that he wasn't keen on the West Highland Way, or simply that he wanted to do something different. He looked tremendously tanned, fit and healthy, and soon left me to stride off at his faster pace.

I came to Cauldstane Slap, slap meaning a gap for sheep and cattle to go through. There was a signpost here, a rarity in this part of Scotland, and a stile, and the flanking East Cairn and West Cairn Hills. I soon descended out of the mist, meeting two cyclists on mountain bikes. Below I could see the waters of Harperrig reservoir, where the path did a squiggle, and I lost it for a time, finding myself with no exit in a field full of sheep. I retreated, to discover yellow painted waymarks on the other side of the wall, which led me to the river crossing at Gala Ford. I had left the Lyne River on the other side of Cauldstane Slap, and these were the headwaters of the Water of Leith which flows to Edinburgh on its way to the Firth of Forth.

I followed a wall down to the main A70 road at Little Vantage, to find myself less than ten miles from Edinburgh, and just a handful of miles along a minor road from my destination, East Calder. This was a real morale-booster; I had in planning thought of East Calder as one important stage of the walk from Kershope, I was now poised to cross the Lowlands by canal towpath to reach the West Highland Way.

The Ordnance Survey seems a bit confused about where East Calder is, with the placename in the middle of a blank space about half a mile from the town proper, but by asking directions

I found my way to Whitecroft Farm, a smallholding and farmshop. This was a warm hospitable place. Mrs Scott had labelled rooms with guests' names, a simple but astonishingly helpful thing to do; it's always difficult when first occupying a room to remember its location. The bathwater was piping hot and the heating was on, too, so I was able to wash my week–old shirt and hang it on the radiator.

I walked into the village and found the fish and chip shop, then took my supper into the recreation ground, but froze, couldn't believe how cold it was after the torrid heat of last week. It was comforting to be back again in the warm of my room.

Outside the farm was a huge horse transport, about the size of a double–decker bus. Mrs Scott told me that there was an important polo match on at the country club down the road, very *posh*, she said. People staying here were in charge of looking after the horses, and she hoped they wouldn't disturb me with their early rising. There was little risk of that, I thought. Sleep comes easily with the end of a day's march.

11: Across the Lowlands.

Sunday May 24th: I followed the minor road just round the corner from Whitecroft, with a signpost at every corner saying Union Canal, until a rough drive led me into a small car-park just by where a high aqueduct led the canal over where the Almond River flowed far below. I soon discovered that I was on the wrong side of the canal; the cobbled towpath which crossed the aqueduct disappeared in thickets of brambles as soon as I reached its far side, and I could see the path going on along the other side of the canal where I needed to be.

I can't even now believe that I was so foolish as to think that there wouldn't be a route to the other side in the absence of a bridge, and to fail to notice that the track which I had left to enter the car park descended to the river then climbed an embankment to reach the far side of the canal. But I didn't notice until I had walked a good mile further to cross the road bridge and walk back a half mile along the north bank. I went on my way knowing that I had added the best part of an hour to the day's march and feeling very annoyed with myself.

I left the canal to cut off a corner as a way of recovering lost time, and had a brief encounter with the main A71 Edinburgh road, busy with Sunday traffic, an unpleasant reminder of civilisation. I took my life in my hands to dart across and ducked into the empty grounds of the Bell refinery. where I huddled behind a hedge to eat lunch.

Back on the canal, I had the wind behind me which was more comfortable, and it felt good to be on what seemed like a highway to the west. Despite my experience of the scenic Kennet and Avon I think I still had the conception of canals as being receptacles for rubbish and the resting place of dead dogs; this can be true, of course, but here the canal flowed between

133

East Calder to Milngavie

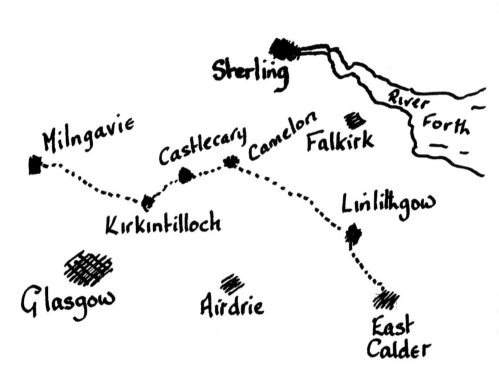

Sterling

River Forth

Milngavie

Castlecary

Camelon

Falkirk

Kirkintilloch

Linlithgow

Glasgow

Airdrie

East Calder

flowering banks and hedges, with a population explosion of waterfowl, swans, mallards and moorhens, each pair with its brood of young. A male swan flapped its wings and hissed menacingly when I came too close for its liking, and another swam protectively around its mate which had somehow become marooned on a piece of floating driftwood and apparently didn't know how to remove itself.

The towers and spires of Linlithgow appeared ahead; I went to the other side of town and found Woodcockdale farm just a hundred yards from the canal bridge on the A706. There was heavy machinery on the canalside and the canal had been drained for a section, work to repair leaks in the canal lining I learned later.

There was a family in the large sitting room at Woodcockdale, an American couple and their two sons from Seattle. They were US Air Force stationed at Lakenheath in Suffolk, but expecting to be posted home after eight years in England following the end of the Cold War. The husband, an American Indian from Alaska and an aircraft technician, spoke of how unprepared he had been for the reality of war in the Desert Storm operation.

I was touched to find Mrs Scott from Whitecroft had telephoned to check on my safe arrival. Monitoring progress I found that today I had completed my first hundred miles from Kershope.

May 25th: Back on the towpath, the sun was breaking through the murk, a beautiful rural setting, may and lilacs in full bloom, no one about. I crossed a magnificent aqueduct over the Avon river seventy feet below, then came into a more populated area, suburban houses just below the embankment and with the roar of the Glasgow–Edinburgh motorway not very distant. On the other side of the canal were high fences surrounding a prison; how quiet it looked, just a closed van outside a building and no sign of human life. I became aware of hurrying to get by.

Near Falkirk the canal was dying; the water was choked with weeds and rubbish and the water fowl had all disappeared. It seemed incongruous that a council employee was tending the canalside verges when the life of the canal was in jeopardy. I came to a town bridge, and found myself at the mouth of a tunnel; I had expected the towpath to climb over, but I saw it disappearing into the darkness.

I realised that I still hadn't replaced the defunct battery in my torch, and decided I was feeling too fragile to trust myself to the gloom without one. I should have to find another way. So I climbed a steep hill and descended flights of steps to arrive at a park–like canalside busy with locals taking the air and people fishing. After a mile the canal ended, just like that, at a spot where it met a minor road.

It had been getting increasingly sultry and a storm was brewing so I hurried along to meet a road complex at Camelon and discover Lock 16 of the Forth and Clyde. This was in the middle of a built–up area, busy with traffic crossing the canal bridge, but the area around the lock had been tidied up and turned into an open space. At its far side was the Union Inn, an historic building dating from the days when it was used for refreshment by bargees while their boats went through the lock.

It was still quite early, but I didn't like the look of the weather, and decided I deserved a rest after two long days; so I asked at the inn about accommodation and was booked without fuss into a commodious self–contained flat, with a view over the canal to fields beyond. I found a small general store across the road and laid in food for supper and tomorrow.

Looking at the map I realised that I had underestimated the distance to Milngavie at the start of the West Highland Way, but it didn't matter too much as I had time in hand and could dawdle over the next two days.

May 26th: A short day, only eight miles, one of them in the wrong direction. The mist was lifting and the air was beautifully fresh after last night's storm. People kept stopping and asking if I was enjoying my walk. I came to a group of men exercising dogs, one, a whippet, racing madly around a field below the towpath. It must be a sign of the times that so many men ap-peared to have time to spare in an area of high unemployment, but I couldn't help thinking that in this sort of weather it's better to be out in the sunshine than grinding in a town. This was a beautiful stretch of canal, with scented May blossom, wild roses coming into bloom, and swans flying to land gracefully on the water; I could hear the beat of their wings sounding like someone tearing soft linen; hush.sh.sh.. they said.

After Bonnybridge the canal was waymarked for a local trail. I came to Underwood Lock, which had been restored; the grass on the verges had been cut short and bright nasturtiums grew in front of the Underwood Lockhouse, an inn and restaurant. The inn was open so I sat in the warm sunshine with a drink enjoying the absence of pressure of time. The canal from here has navigable stretches and is used extensively for pleasure cruising after years of neglect, although restoration for the whole of its length would be expensive, as continuous access has been interrupted by new road bridges.

At Castlecary there was an unbelievably squalid and littered picnic site under the bridge where traffic on the main A80 trunk road roared by. I hastily left the clamour behind and walked into Banknock to telephone for accommodation, only to find that I had to walk back a mile to the same noise and pollution to find a way over the main road and under a railway viaduct to Castle-cary village. I found Wayside Lodge up a cul-de-sac, to be warmly welcomed with tea and friendly talk.

27th May: I walked through the neighbouring trading estate and crossed the line of the Antonine Wall. This was built by the Romans in the second century AD as the Empire's most northerly line of defence. The wall is not so well preserved as its counterpart Hadrian's Wall, but traces of it remain just up the road from Castlecary. I went on to the canal and came across a class of schoolchildren with their teachers busily fishing for material for their field studies and poring over muddy water in washing-up bowls. A boat came by loaded with noisy excited older children, one of them steering erratically.

The wild-life was back with a vengeance, with the population explosion continuing. A pen was sitting on a huge nest built of reeds with her mate swimming around, and broods of young followed their parents in line astern. The canal was opening out into wider basins and becoming more sea-like, with the brisk east wind whipping up ripples, rather harsh and unsettling coming from a cloudless sky. I recognised the line of hills sketched on the northern horizon as the Campsie Fells, Glasgow's own personal hills, and realised I was within reach of the West

Highland Way.

Near Kirkintilloch the industrial nature of the Lowlands reasserted itself, with a network of roads visible on both sides of the canal embankment. I looked across the wide valley to the north where earsplitting crashes were coming from a hillside quarry. There was the sight, rare for me, of double–decker buses and lines of traffic drawn up at a road junction.

Kirkintilloch was having its road system reorganised with accompanying chaos, but someone directed me to the Broadcroft Hotel, apparently the only accommodation in the district. This had clearly been built as a conference centre and was not a walker's kind of place, but it was a case of any port in a storm. I booked in and went to look at the town, which was quite nice, built around the canal, with an old church and accessible shopping centre so I did some essential shopping before returning to eat in the hotel dining–room. This had a superb view over the Campsie Fells, and the east wind, blowing out of the same clear sky, was battering the picture windows.

May 28th: Breakfast service was willing but incompetent; I had to keep asking for things, tea, a spoon for my egg, and milk for my tea when it came – and for double the cost of B&B. I went back to follow the canal for three miles to Cadder, crossed the river Kelvin and then the main road, where green and yellow buses had Glasgow as their destination. I went on along little rambling farm roads, with hills to climb, a novelty after the horizontal towpath. To the north were views of distant hills emerging as if coming out of developing fluid, to the south the skyscrapers of Glasgow.

I crossed a shallow ford and then the second golf course of the day, thinking how like my own corner of Kent and that this must be the subtopian side of Glasgow with its large well–cared for houses and open spaces, then descended a steep hill into town. I liked Milngavie (pronounced Mul–guy) straight away, with its traffic–free shopping centre, and air of unhurried busyness. Almost at once I found the marker board directing me on to the West Highland Way, at a point where a little alleyway left the shopping precinct. I felt eager to start this next important section of my walk, which would take me into the Highlands, but I'd

138

booked B&B in Milngavie, so went off to find Craig Dhu Avenue.

It rained that evening, with thunder rumbling to the south; rain was needed for the gardens, said Mrs Ogilvie. I had walked into town to buy fish and chips for supper and sheltered under a tree to eat them; all the teashops were shut and the restaurants opened later, but fish and chips are nice enough and cheap.

Mrs Ogilvie had done the West Highland Way with her husband, and gave me advice I was to hear again, to allow plenty of time for the Loch Lomond section; I thought there was no risk of my not doing. I hadn't actually broken any records along the canals but it would be nice to be in hill country again, and I did have plenty of time, not having to be in Fort William until June 7th.

I was coming to appreciate that the reality of walking a section of route can never be as anticipated in the planning however thorough the reading of guidebooks and studying of maps. In the event, so many more variables have to be counted in: the weather, season of the year, people met along the way, your own state of well-being or otherwise, all these will be part of the memories of any walking trip of whatever length. There's a sense of discovery in being in a place for the first time, an experience which won't be repeated. So after completing a section I was coming to recognise a sensation of loss, a feeling of never again. Returning to somewhere once visited is like watching an action replay or the repeat of a film; it will still be enjoyable but different in that the feeling of confronting something strange and unfamiliar will have disappeared.

Fort William
Ben Nevis
Loch Leven
Kinlochleven
Loch Linnhe
Devil's Staircase
Kingshouse Hotel
Loch Tulla
Bridge of Orchy
Tyndrum
Inveroran
Auchtertye
Crianlarich
Loch Katrine
Inversnaid
Ferry
Rowardennan
Loch Lomond
Milton
Drymen
Milngavie

12 : Taking the High Road

To start along the West Highland Way is really to feel on a highway to the north. Not all long distance paths are like that; the Cotswold Way never seems to be quite sure of its direction. The Pennine Way is better, but a walker crossing from Teesdale will end the day at Dufton further away from Kirk Yetholm than at the start. Owain Glyndwr's Way crosses mid–Wales in an easterly direction before doing a U–turn to finish at its starting point, Machynlleth.

The West Highland Way, by contrast, makes no bones about where it is heading; from the start there's a real feeling of getting somewhere. The route gradually detaches itself from the Lowlands, taking a line which leads from the Glasgow suburbs into tamed wood–land where families take their weekend exercise, past the lower shores of Loch Lomond, a waterside resort for Glaswegians. From there the country becomes rougher and lonelier, the hills higher, and the scenery grander, until the highest point of the Way is reached at the summit of the Devil's Staircase. The West Highland Way ends at the foot of Britain's highest mountain, Ben Nevis.

For all its grandeur, the Way takes a line of least resistance, leading through glens and over passes. Near Crianlarich, about halfway to Fort William, the Way climbs on to an old military road, which it follows for many of the miles thereafter. This road in its turn is using ancient drove roads, giving firm footing and safe direction, and offering glimpses of growing splendour in the landscape.

If, like me, you intend to go north beyond Fort William, there is the feeling of greater things yet to come and choices to be made, for there is more than one way leading to Cape Wrath. It is like travelling along the course of a great river and coming to the point at which it divides into a number of branching tributaries. Once embarked on one of these there is no going back.

I had made my choices, it seemed long ago in the security of my home. I would head through the outskirts of Knoydart into Wester Ross and some trackless country through high hills, keeping as far as possible to my northerly direction up the middle of Scotland. I would finally reach the wild and lonely northern county of Sutherland which would lead to Cape Wrath. I was feeling a mixture of excitement and apprehension about these final stages of the walk; there would be times when the day would end in a tent rather than in the comfort of B&B and my resolution would be tested by the weather, midges, and my own physical resources. It would also mean reacquaintance with some of the most beautiful country to be found anywhere in the British Isles. I was eager to be there and glad that I would have companions for these final miles.

May 29th: It was good to be heading north, leaving the town in Scotch misty sort of weather, soon clearing to hot sunshine. I began to enjoy myself straight away, relishing the views of the approaching hills. The backache which had been bothering me all along the canals had disappeared; I decided it preferred the hills.

I came over a rise to a real picture–postcard scene, a splendid view of Dungoyne at the end of the Campsie Fells rising above a calm loch. Two backpackers overtook me and we walked together for a while, the first time I had met other walkers since the Pentlands. The path, well provided with waymarks, led across open country, winding round the wooded volcanic landmark of Dumgoyach. Sooner than expected the route turned on the track of the disused Blane Valley Railway, which is followed for four miles. I stopped to eat a protracted lunch in hot sunshine.

I came into Drymen and found the village busy with visitors. This was the weekend of the Drymen Show, and accommodation was at a premium. I found my way to my B&B on Stirling Road, where, accepting the usual offer of tea I was ushered into a homely kitchen crowded with people, Mr and Mrs Lander, their two teenage children, and another couple of guests, Germans from Frankfurt also on their first day of the West Highland Way.

The children were just celebrating their final day of public examinations, a reminder to me that school holidays were still to come.

May 30th: A day off walking. I left my rucksack and collected a parcel from the Post Office; the guidebook says that the village, small by south of England standards, offers shops and services not matched until Kinlochleven a hundred kilometres further on. 'The walker will do well to look to his purse.' I bought ballpoint pens to replace those I had already lost, changed my socks and posted a parcel home, then walked the mile down the road to the Buchanan Estate where the show was being held, my hosts having urged me to visit their biggest event of the year.

I paid £1 entrance and found a scene I'd in the past seen only on the TV screen; it was hard to believe I hadn't strayed on to the set of Horse of the Year Show. In one part of the huge field horses were being put through their paces over hurdles, in another shire horses were being judged. Beautifully groomed Angus and Charollais bulls tethered behind cattle transporters waited patiently for their turn in the ring. In another place a spectacular exhibition of trampolining was going on, wonderfully lissom and agile young people executing impossibly intricate leaps and somersaults. A kilted pipe band played. All this within a external perimeter of displays of farm machinery and stalls selling all manner of food and drink.

After a while I walked back to Stirling Road and found the Germans taking the sun in the garden. By a stroke of bad luck one of the couple had sprained an ankle yesterday, and her foot had turned an impressive shade of purple, so they were resting it before continuing their walk. Mrs Lander came back from the show and made tea and we all relaxed until it was time for me to go. I called in to the Spa grocer's to buy supper then walked the two miles along the road to Milton of Buchanan and my B&B for the night.

May 31st: I left out the swathe of the West Highland Way over Conic Hill and walked along the road to Balmaha, to reach the bonnie banks of Loch Lomond. It was going to be a scorching day, and the lochside resembled the Cote d'Azur, with camping and caravan sites, paddlers, power boats and water skiers. The

West Highland Way soon showed its teeth, leaving the road to climb steeply through woods and descending just as steeply to meet the road from time to time. There traffic was hurtling round the blind bends, not the kind of walking I particularly enjoyed, but there were exciting views of approaching hills.

I found a beautiful still lochan to settle by for lunch, until the midges found me and drove me on, so I reached Rowardennan and its youth hostel early. West Highland Way walkers and others were gathering from all directions and the hostel was full. The YHA has changed since the days fifty years ago when spartan conditions were supposed to be part of the pleasure of outdoor holidays. Nowadays rules have been relaxed and comforts such as showers and TV are taken for granted, while the use of cars is no longer sternly proscribed and water sports and outdoor activities such as para–gliding are catered for. So the clientele included people who had driven out for the weekend from the big towns as well as bona fide long–distance walkers.

The hostel cooks surely enjoyed their work, and supper was the best meal I'd had since leaving home, good home–made soup, steak and mushroom pie, and luscious cheesecake. There was an assortment of friendly walkers of all ages, some already nursing sore feet and blisters. People were talking apprehensively about the next section of the walk along Loch Lomond. For those using hostels the next stage involved a twenty–two mile stretch to Crianlarich along some of the most difficult terrain of the Way. I was glad I wasn't under that kind of pressure, but started to worry about accommodation, which became difficult from here.

It rained, a heavy thundery shower, and after the rain stopped came the midges in swarms, invading the hostel through open doors and windows. No escaping the fact that I was in Scotland! *June 1st:* Along with a number of other hostellers I took the upper forest track rather than the more difficult route along the loch–shore, easily to the end of the forest road, and still driven on by the midges. I was getting bitten despite hat, midge repellent and mosquito net. And in the increasing heat flies were joining in the feast. The going became rough, the path climbing and descending repeatedly, across numerous small streams, and through black mud. I sweated and laboured, feeling trapped between the lochshore on the one hand and the steep mountainside on the other, without any means of escape, and was glad to emerge at the bridge over the famous falls at Inversnaid.

Outside the hotel was another gathering of Way walkers fortifying themselves for the next stage to Inverarnan. With no prospect of a bed between here and Crianlarich I was ending my day's walk early, so booked into the hotel, which was even more crowded than the YHA, with four coach parties on package holidays. I took my book outside to find a quiet corner and look at the view, which was lovely, the loch mirror–smooth and the clouds beginning to enfold the hills. I was driven indoors by the evening shower, which I hoped wasn't becoming too much of a habit.

June 2nd: I took the ferry across Loch Lomond to Inveruglas, along with about thirty members of a coach party. This was stretching Rule One a bit but I was feeling fragile after a disturbed night, and didn't like the look of the weather. Disembarking, I set off along the road which wasn't at all bad. The early morning thunderstorm had cleared the air, and I made good progress to Ardlui, where I was able to replenish my supplies of bananas and goodies at the well–stocked shop.

I caught up with the West Highland Way at Inverarnan, where the hotel was firmly closed, and there was a plethora of Way–walkers going in both directions. The path led resolutely around a field and across numerous stiles so as to shield walkers from the gaze of farm–dwellers, then joined a track leading into Glen Falloch and ascending gently to follow the course of the river, an easy afternoon's walk, eventually to emerge on the main A82 road and climb steeply to join Wade's military road, which I was going to be following for many of the remaining miles to Fort William. As soon as I reached the open hillside, unconstrained by the river valley, I felt more at ease with the landscape; big hills were coming into view, wreathed in cloud on this rather murky day, but telling me I was really in the Highlands.

I left the track to descend into Crianlarich and the station where I telephoned for a bed; the second call brought an offer of a lift up the road to the Lodge, a large comfortable house half a mile from town. I settled in and went down to the lounge to see who was there, and to my amazement found Ron Roweth ensconced. Ron and I had last seen each other three weeks ago, in Sevenoaks, when he had been organising a hundred mile walk for the Long Distance Walkers Association and I had been helping with drinks points and supporting Dick who was doing the walk. Ron was staying in the district with his sights set on the high hills, but had with a friend completed the West Highland Way last year, so we had much to talk about.

The Lodge was full, with a touring American couple and another party of walkers. Supper was good, lentil soup and trout in oatmeal, and I began to feel better fed, after a rather uncertain diet in the early stages. It was encouraging, too, to talk about my plans with someone as experienced as Ron, who knew Scotland well.

June 3rd: Ron walked with me back into Crianlarich then went on to add Ben More and Stobinian to his tally of hills climbed. I recovered lost height to reach the deer fence where I had left the West Highland Way yesterday. I wasn't too sure where I would spend tonight; Tyndrum was a short seven miles ahead, but didn't seem to have any vacancies, and to go on to Bridge of Orchy a further seven miles would put me too far ahead of schedule. I decided to follow my nose and see what happened.

It was turning into a fine day, the murk which had been hanging about all yesterday lifting, and views opening up everywhere, back across Crianlarich to the Ben More massif, and forward to hills overlooking Glen Fillan. The track stayed high for a time before descending to cross the main road and into farming country.

I followed the farm road to skirt farm buildings and came to Auchtertye, with a B&B sign outside a farm cottage. It was still early in the day, but I needed to do shopping and sort out accommodation for the rest of the way to Fort William, so I booked in, left my rucksack, and walked the mile into Tyndrum. The village was thriving and busy with holidaymakers, with a good general store, so I shopped and did some productive tele-phoning and had coffee in the large teashop. I walked back by the 'improved' road, which had unpleasantly fast traffic.

June 4th: The West Highland Way into Tyndrum was distinctly better than the road. I climbed over a col and around the back of the village, then struck along the line of the old road to Bridge of Orchy, with the accompaniment of the scenic west coast railway, which had never been very far away since the end of Loch Lomond. It was an exhilarating walk into the mountains, with the weather its Scottish best, sunny, fluffy white clouds, not too hot. I went under the railway by a cattle–creep where people were excavating with pick–axes and came to a farm where the railway did one of its famous U–turns to cross the Kinglass river; a train came by as I was sitting by the wayside having second breakfast, and two or three groups of way–walkers overtook me.

Someone came up behind me and a voice said, 'Are you a long–distance walker?' It was another surprise meeting, Kevin and Jackie, acquaintances from Kent, so we walked together until they stopped for lunch, to overtake me again on the section over Mam Carraigh to Inverornan. By now it was sweatingly hot and the flies were coming out in the forest, but more exciting views opened out as we came over the pass. Ahead was Loch Tulla with the imposing buildings of Black Mount Lodge framed by trees on its far side. To the north and west rose the craggy hills of the Black Mount, dark summits whose names I did not know. To the north–east the main road skirted the watery bounds of the Moor of Rannoch.

We descended the hillside to the white buildings of the Inverornan Hotel immediately below. I was staying here, Jackie and Kevin waiting for transport to a farm some miles off–route.

We assembled for drinks in the bar, where a small group of walkers had gathered in a friendly atmosphere. The two–hundred–year–old hotel was a nice wee place, small enough to seem homely despite what seemed an excessive number of prohibitions, don't put rucksacks on bed, wash clothes in your room, go behind the bar, etc.; perhaps this was from experience of walker behaviour in the past, although most of the prohibited activities seemed harmless enough. I hoped washing smalls didn't count, as this was a nightly ritual for me.

I had supper in the bar and sat in the lounge afterwards with two West Highland Way walkers, who gave me a replacement ball–point when my own ran out. My fame must have spread, are you the woman who's walked from the Border? I was asked. I noted that today I had passed two hundred miles, which on mileage alone would make me half–way to Cape Wrath, but it isn't like that in Scotland, since map miles mean nothing in the kind of trackless wastes I was to meet later.

June 5th: It was another glorious morning, promising to be hot; I walked round the head of Loch Tulla to climb again by the old road, with splendid views of the peaks around the vast recesses of Coire Ba to the west and the water–logged expanse of Rannoch Moor to the east. I kept stopping to look at the emerging views as I climbed, descended to Ba Bridge, and climbed again to the high point of the road at 1450 feet. Ba Bridge was smaller than I expected, just a little packhorse arch dating from the days of the old drove road; two people were taking the sun where a tent was pitched on a grassy sward by the river.

As I climbed, more peaks appeared to the north and east. A triangular peak appearing between nearer hills as a blue sketch on the skyline, almost a mirage, I recognised as Schiehallion, the fairy hill of the Caledonians. I remembered my first sight of this magic mountain, seen from the train which crosses the Moor of Rannoch. I had been on my first visit to the Highlands in the aftermath of a failed relationship, and the sight of Schiehallion marked the beginning of a lifelong love affair with Scotland which has grown stronger over the years. I was not, even so, to stand on Schiehallion's summit for more than thirty years; somehow the hill had always been by–passed on the way to other remoter peaks in the north–west, until in 1981 on the way home from a holiday in the Outer Hebrides there was a day to spare. We camped in a hidden spot near Amulree, drove to Braes of Foss, and climbed the worn path to the summit. Dick nearly trod on an adder sunning itself on the peaty ground, and fifteen–year–old Robert, impatient with our slow pace, dashed ahead on the descent to make tea in the car.

There were more memories to come as the track began to descend, and the portals of Glencoe unfolded. With theatrical suddenness the great pyramid of Buchaille Etive Mor, the shepherd of Glen Etive, emerged beyond the craggy flanks of Meall a' Bhuiridh. Far ahead miniature cars sped along the road into Glencoe, and across the watery expanse of the moor I could see the white shape of the Kingshouse Hotel. I sat by the trackside to look at the view; two kilted Scots came along, one immensely large, his stomach escaping over the top of his kilt. He was massively encumbered with camping gear, pots and pans and various bundles hanging from his already overladen rucksack. His companion was more spare in girth and equipment. I followed them downhill, to cross the main road, and reach the hotel.

I ordered tea, and telephoned to Kinlochleven where I was to spend the night; Kingshouse was full and I should have to return here tomorrow to complete the next stage. The hotel was busy with walkers and motorists; the two women I had shared B&B with at Tyndrum were there and were going to the same place at Kinlochleven, but finishing the walk there today. Outside on the terrace a man was instructing his wife in the use of a Camcorder: 'You press the red button dear, but wait until I've finished speaking...'. Some sheep were picking their way delicately across the stones of the nearly dried-up river below.

After a while Bob Ledson drove up and we set off down the glen, stopping after a while to say hello to the two walkers who were about to start the climb over the Devil's Staircase. We drove between well-remembered hills, the Stob Dearg of Buchaille Etive Mor, the buttresses of the Three Sisters of Glencoe guarding the higher slopes of Bidean nam Bian, the jagged teeth of the Aonach Eagach. We passed the Signal Rock, the point where the command to begin the Massacre of Glencoe was given. Memories of this act of mass murder in 1691 are especially acute because of its betrayal of hospitality; the troops carrying out the massacre were quartered on the villagers. It is said that those bearing the associated name of Campbell are still unwelcome in Glencoe.

Levenside House was at the end of a drive fringed with rhododendrons, its tangled garden falling down the hillside to the end of Loch Leven. I settled in then walked into town to look for food. The restaurant was closed but the fish and chip shop advertised frying while you wait, so I bought my fish and chips and sat outside in the late sunshine to eat them. I was by now becoming something of an authority on fish and chips and I decided that these must without doubt be the best in Scotland. The fish was mouth–wateringly fresh and flaky, and coated with crisp dry batter, with a generous helping of equally tasty chips.

My brother–in–law John Timmins told me later of hurtling down to Kinlochleven from the Blackwater Dam after a twenty–mile walk, and carrying a dozen portions of fish and chips the five hundred feet uphill to Mamore Lodge where his walking club were staying.

Bob Ledson was ready early next morning to drive me back to Kingshouse; he had the previous year walked the West Highland Way for charity dressed in Loch Ness Monster costume, and had reassuring things to say about the walk over the Devil's Staircase, which sounded daunting but wasn't. Bob had an interesting history; hailing from Liverpool, he had travelled the world in the Army before moving to Scotland and the accommodation business, but was contemplating moving back to England in the wake of recent redundancy and falling off of tourist trade. Apart from people packing a handful of resorts, it was noticeable how few holiday–makers were around, and there was a marked absence of foreign cars.

June 6th: We arrived at Kingshouse to find it a hive of activity, cars and tents everywhere, and athletic–looking young people purposefully limbering up. I discovered that a triathlon was starting from the hotel, a mixture of cycling, canoeing and running. This would be strenuous in the extreme on what was going to be a scorcher of a day.

I was heading in the opposite direction, and set off lightly laden having been able to leave some gear at Kinlochleven. The route still clung to the old military road which I had been following since Crianlarich, built in the eighteenth century largely as a response to the Jacobite uprisings of 1715 and 1745. It is a tribute to the builders that so many miles of the military road remain in good condition and form highroads into the hills.

I followed the West Highland Way as a faint track around the slopes of Beinn a'Chrulaiste, then along the level to join the busy Glencoe road at Altnafeadh. The Devil's Staircase path begins here, apparently christened so by the road's builders, although

150

strictly the name only applies to the well engineered zig–zags which lead to the summit of the pass over to Kinlochleven. On this summer morning there was nothing particularly demonic about this fine mountain walk, except for the heat, which was becoming intense. A party of four day–walkers overtook me and we proceeded to leap–frog each other as we toiled up the steep part to reach the summit, at 1450 feet the highest point of the Way.

At the cairn an exciting view unfolded to the north dominated by the unmistakable hulk of Ben Nevis flanked by the mountains and ridges of the Mamore Forest. Below Nevis, one and a half days' walk from here was Fort William, and another important stage of my walk would have been completed.

The descent to Kinlochleven gave ample time for looking at the view, of the Blackwater reservoir to the North–east, and the craggy Leven valley unfolding below. It seemed to take a long time, as the track contoured along the hillside, to join the water–works road at the spot where the great pipes from Blackwater plunge down the steep hillside to carry water to power the aluminium smelter at Kinlochleven, which is the reason for the town's existence.

The road descended steeply into a wooded valley. where I stopped to rest in the shade. A young backpacker came along in the opposite direction, heavily laden but looking tanned and fit. I was thrilled to discover that he had walked from Cape Wrath and was heading for his home in Falmouth, Cornwall. He spoke glowingly of the far north, of the wonderful solitude of being in the wilderness, and made me want to be there myself.

A group of six women came along, nursing staff who were doing a sponsored walk in aid of their work–place, a hospice in Ayr. They were survivors of a group of sixteen who had started three days ago; I decided I couldn't be doing too badly. We walked together into Kinlochleven, where Bob Ledson met me at the door; 'You've been running,' he said accusingly. It wasn't true, of course, but made me feel good.

June 7th: Another scorcher; after the descent of more than a thousand feet to sea level at Kinlochleven there's an equivalent climb out of the town, up a steep hillside through birchwoods, a steady climb needing stops to admire the view of the deep-set fiord-like loch with its surround of shapely hills. The party from Ayr overtook me and went ahead at a good pace, with transport to meet in Fort William.

The path debouched on the main track at the top of the hill, and the angle eased, with the Glencoe hills occupying the southern horizon, and the Mamore ridge rising to the north. I looked back to trace the route down from Devil's Staircase, now falling behind. The glen became more enclosed and barren as I reached the summit of the Lairigmor pass and descended to pass the ruin of Lairigmor. I stopped to eat my packed lunch, and a group of four walkers stopped to take my photograph, they'd heard of me they said.

The track descended from the bare hills once for all and joined a hot and stony forestry road for a long mile to meet the little metalled public road. The West Highland Way proper strikes over the hill to descend into Glen Nevis, but the way was barred by tapes and a notice saying the path was closed for tree-felling and re-directing walkers down the road.

There were a few cars in the small Forestry Commission car park, and people sunning themselves by the river. I went on along the quiet road in the afternoon heat, the road climbing and descending to small hamlets and farms, with only the occasional car to disturb the peace. There was a final climb to reach the viewpoint where the sea-loch and Fort William were spread below, with Ben Nevis now displaying its hugh bulk to the east, such an unusual sight to have the highest mountain in Britain crystal clear, not a cloud to obscure its summit.

I hadn't booked anywhere to stay; spending three nights in Fort William, I wanted to choose my accommodation carefully. I was, all the same, feeling uncomfortably hot and sweaty and ready to rest, so decided as I descended the steep road, that I would choose the first likely place that would have me.

Abrach House was a modern building set on the hillside over-looking Loch Linnhe. Charlie Moore greeted me at the door, and I immediately decided that this would do nicely, a relaxed homely atmosphere and all necessary creature comforts. So I set-tled in and looked forward to a spell of doing nothing very much.

Interlude

Fort William is an important stage on a walk through Scotland, marking the south–western extremity of the Great Glen, the massive fault line which cuts the country in two between east and west coasts. The Caledonian Canal built by Telford still gives access to both North Sea and Atlantic coasts for sea–going vessels. The quality of the countryside changes north of the Great Glen, becoming less accessible, wilder and with obstacles to easy travel posed by high mountains and large areas of water, Scottish lochs and sea–lochs which dictate how roads, tracks and walkers thread their way northwards. This is particularly so if taking a route up the west side; not too far from Fort William to the north–west are the rough bounds of Knoydart, their spectacular peaks seen by car–bound travellers from the viewpoint on the new road which climbs above Glengarry towards Shiel Bridge. Travellers in the rough bounds must be self–sufficient, using tent or bothy.

Beyond Shiel Bridge is more wilderness, a vast area of mountainous country, some of it trackless, leading to the hills of Torridon, and, beyond, to the remote Letterewe and Fisherfield Forests. I had saved this country for the latter stages of the walk because I knew from earlier visits of its beauty and solitude; it seemed right to keep the best until last. I had chosen, too, to aim for Cape Wrath going as far as possible up the centre of Scotland, although it will be seen that this did not necessarily mean aiming due north, the lie of the land often deciding the direction of travel.

Fort William, then, was a good place to take stock, and to prepare for the rough country which lay ahead. It was here, too, that I was to end the solo walking. Dick was to walk with me for a few days, then our daughter Caroline would take over as travelling companion. Up to now plans had worked out well, and I had achieved the goals I had set for myself in terms of distance travelled; I was still wondering how I would cope with the wilderness.

Abrach House was a nice place to be, friendly and informal. Charlie Moore did most of the main organisation of the house, his wife being head of music at the local secondary school. The household was augmented by a teenage daughter and an African grey parrot, the second I had encountered in Scotland. This one was a temporary guest, belonging to Charlie's mother–in–law, who was away in Canada; he could often be found walking about the house and 'helping' Charlie with the gardening, his whistle and incessant chatter quite unmistakable.

The house, perched on the hillside, had splendid views over Loch Linnhe, to the hills and glen opposite. On the first evening I looked down on Fort William and its harbour, to see the lights come on in the calm grey dusk; a two–masted barque cruised majestically down the loch.

In a generally quiet summer Abrach House was busy with guests, people using it as a base for travel and sight–seeing, and others like me finishing the West Highland Way. Guests included an ex–fighter pilot who had served at Biggin Hill in the Battle of Britain, and two walkers from Whitby who were also railway buffs and had extensive knowledge of the Waverly line I had walked along earlier.

The two days passed quickly; I did the reorganising which had to be done, and on the first day went into town to buy a sleeping bag, something I had promised myself to replace my thirty–year-old Black's Icelandic. Not wanting to tempt providence I had deliberately chosen to leave this essential purchase until I knew I would have imminent need of it. I went to West Coast Sports-wear in the High Street to find the three–season 'Softie', weighing not much more than a kilogram, which I had spotted in the London YHA shop. I found myself telling the friendly assistant why I needed a lightweight sleeping bag, and felt in saying it that I had committed myself finally to the last stage of the journey.

Fort William was crowded with an assortment of locals, young people in walking gear, and oldies on coach tours. I wondered where I fitted in. I met four people I had last seen at Bridge of Orchy, who had arrived in Fort William a day ahead of me. They had climbed Nevis the previous day in perfect weather. The guidebook says that climbing Nevis is a fitting conclusion to the West Highland Way, but I had no ambition to repeat an ascent made over thirty years earlier.

I went into town next day to look at the West Highland Museum, a converted house in the square next to the tourist information, a good forty pence worth for pensioners. The place was crammed with historic material ancient and modern, with a particularly full account of the 1745 rebellion and its aftermath. The past seems very close in this corner of Scotland, where just along the Great Glen is Achnacarry, where Cameron of Lochiel, who fought with the Young Pretender, had his house, and where his descendants still live.

There were exhibits on major construction works, the Caledonian Canal, and more recently the Ballachulish Bridge over the narrows between Lochs Linnhe and Leven. People of my generation remember the days when there was a choice between waiting in a queue for the ferry or driving round the head of the loch via Kinlochleven. I looked at the clothing and tartans and marvelled at the still vibrant greens and reds, wondering how in past centuries people were able to dye cloth in a way which would not fade with time.

I returned to Abrach House to sew on buttons, and after supper walked down to the station; I was early for the Glasgow train so paused at the Parade Gardens to watch and listen to a pipe band. Bagpipe music seems supremely suited to the open air. The train arrived on time to the minute, and out stepped Dick, who had had a ten–hour journey from London, and would be walking with me for the next four days.

Cluanie Bridge
Loch Cluanie
Loch Loyne
Loch Garry
Tomdoun Hotel
Loch Lochy
Chia-aig Falls
Gairlochy
Banavie
Fort William

Fort William to Cluanie

13: Over the hills and far away

Wednesday June 10th: Time to move on; we spent the morning doing sorting out and I did some drastic weeding of my luggage, managing to pack a two–kilo parcel to leave space to accommodate my new sleeping bag, which I hadn't even dared to remove from its stuff sac. Such things are like the proverbial can of worms in being easier to remove than to replace so best left alone until needed.

We left bidding a grateful farewell to Charlie who said on learning of our destination 'I've never *walked* to Banavie.' Put that way it's easy to see why people think it's rather odd to insist on walking every step of the way through rather uninspiring streets when there's perfectly adequate public transport. It was only four miles, but crossing the Caledonian Canal to Banavie would give us a start for next day.

The murk had been burned away, and it was becoming too hot for comfort; with no need to hurry we dawdled along, finding plenty to look at in the changing views of Nevis as we threaded our way through the suburbs; a track by the railway took us to Inverlochy Castle and a river crossing, and we spent an extended lunch break basking in the sun. A minor road brought us to the Caledonian Canal at Neptune's Staircase, a flight of eight locks which raises the canal the seventy feet from sea level. We looked at and admired the machinery for opening the lock gates, still in working order although electricity has replaced horsepower.

That was our day really; we walked up the road to our B&B and room with a grandstand view of Nevis, which like many hills best displays its grandeur to mortals gazing from the plains.

June 11th: Back to Neptune's Staircase on another cloudless morning, to follow the canal towpath. The Caledonian canal can't boast the wealth of wildfowl found on the Forth and

Clyde, the River Lochy visible to our right below the embanked canal affording a safer haven. There was still much to see in the variety of craft using the waterway, a motor launch, a fishing smack Posidiana from Hull flying the red duster, and a holiday barge from Holland. We were to catch up with all these waiting at the lock and swing bridge at Gairlochy, where a seaman greeted us with a comment about the tortoise and the hare. We were equally interested in the notice directing us to the Stables tearoom on the other side of the lock. We sat outside in the sun against a hedge smothered in roses and could have believed ourselves to be in the South of France.

We left the canal to take the minor road to Achnacarry mercifully under tree–cover in the blistering heat through deciduous woods of oak, sycamore, beech, copper beech and mountain ash, and some huge mature spruce. We took the path past the estate church, where we stopped in the shade to lunch. The tiny church was open where in the south so many are locked for security, and we looked inside and found the little vestry at the top of the spiral staircase.

The path brought us out by the entrance to Achnacarry Castle, the traditional home of the Cameron Clan, twice destroyed by fire, once in revenge after the forty–five rebellion and then in wartime when it was headquarters for the Commando Corps. There were a few houses and a tiny post–office. We walked along to cross the bridge at the outlet to Loch Arkaig and join the road which wends its way to the end of the loch, the way into Knoydart.

We turned down the road to reach the bridge over Chia–aig river where tomorrow's walk to Tomdoun would start. Today we were returning to Gairlochy for our night's bed and board, so started to look around for a lift.

There were one or two cars parked near the bridge but little other traffic on this dead–end road, but after a while a car with Netherland plates stopped. The driver, indicating the crammed rear seat, said he could only take us 'in emergency', and seemed to accept our assurance that the alternative of a seven–mile walk could qualify. We piled in, and as we went the driver told us that this was his first visit to England since 1944, when he had been recruited after the liberation of Holland to train as a Commando; he was here now because he wanted to show his wife the area. We asked what it had been like, and he told us of survival and assault training and of long route marches with sixty–pound pack, but said 'I'm still alive', had suffered no harm, and 'you do at twenty what you wouldn't do forty years later'.

Back at Gairlochy, where we left our benefactors, a large naval vessel was just about to enter the lock. It was a fisheries protection vessel crossing from the North Sea, very spick and span with crew lined up on the upper deck and signal flags flying. It looked huge in the confines of the lock, only inches from its side.

From our window at Heatherlea we saw Nevis still in view, with snow lying in the gullies of its north face, and the canal basin was mirror smooth in the evening light as we walked back up the hill from our evening meal at Stables. Scottish late tea is a much–appreciated custom, and we shared it with another guest, a researcher from Aberdeen University, who was doing a survey of deer population in the forests; he spoke feelingly of the monster clegs, or horse–flies, which plagued his days.

June 12th: Promised to be another scorcher. We had a lift to our starting point, the waterfall bridge at Chia–aig and embarked along the route of a waymarked scenic walk, with the steep climb from the road well protected with steps and guardrails against the drop to the gorge below. There was a thousand feet of climbing in shade to the point where the waymarked path returned to the road by a different route. We left it to follow the forest track to where it ended in a turning place and was replaced by a muddy path which soon brought us to the edge of the forest at a stile. Stopping for a breather we were overtaken by a couple on their way to climb one of the hills we were approaching. They were followed by a party of ten pony–trekkers bound for Tomdoun; we declined their offer of a spare mount, and spent the next hour repelling the clegs gathering in their path.

The path led out onto the open hillside and crossed a river; we noted that the bridge marked on the map had seen better days and with the river so low it seemed safer to hop across. After that the path more or less disappeared, leaving us to pick our way across the drumlins. These are moraine ridges, debris deposited by the glaciers as they cut their way down the valleys. It had turned into one–mile–an–hour country and hot to boot.

We came at last to the ruined croft at Fedden, where the path ended; we crossed the river, and a line of peat hags to the opposite hillside looking for the next track to take us over the watershed. I ran out of fuel before Dick, and lagged behind as we climbed too high before deciding that the track must lie below us. But we were rewarded by seeing deer and a splendid view of the Knoydart hills to the northwest; nose–high against the angle of ascent I came across a clump of the star–like Grass of Parnassus. We stayed high to eat lunch then contoured to join the path we could see below.

The track soon deteriorated, obscured by new planting, and we followed a forest fence for what seemed like hours. The ground had been turned over by machinery into ankle–wrenching lumps, and a number of small water–courses made runnels in it. The motor–cycle rally which uses this route seemed to have made its marks too in the ruts which scored the ground, and the passing ponies had added their contribution. Hot, sweaty and tired, we went through a gate to reach a real forestry track and a clear route down to Greenfield. It was a long way, and even with midges gathering and discouraging any lengthy halt it was seven in the evening when we crossed the bridge over Loch Garry and reached the road, with two and a half miles to go to the Tomdoun Hotel.

I was feeling more tired than I liked after a strenuous day, so suggested to Dick that he go on at his own pace to the hotel; he could have first bath and make sure of a meal, so off he went at his best long distance walker's pace. I sat by the roadside attempting to summon up what remained of my strength, and after a while plodded on, trying to concentrate on other things than aching back and legs, like the view across the loch, which was superb, and the flowers by the verges, and the prospect of a long hot soak in a large bath. After a while I met a party of young people, who greeted me cheerfully and said the hotel 'wasn't far', then the driver of a large estate car stopped to say hello; it was packed with our pony–trekking friends, who had put

160

their mounts out to grass and were on their way to the hotel, which did indeed turn out to be just round the corner. I liked the Tomdoun Hotel, which was unpretentious and unfussy, and gave us lovely baked trout and salad for supper. I was ready to collapse in a heap after finishing mine and even the noise from the pony–trekking party having a good time couldn't keep me awake. I fell into a deep well of sleep.

June 13th: Somewhere a few days back we had seen a weather forecast which promised rain by Saturday, which was today, and there was every sign of its accuracy in low overcast and mist descending on the peaks with the wind in the south–west. The day started with a three–mile road walk, and along the way we met a couple walking in from Barrisdale, the bothy by Loch Hourn in Knoydart. We asked them about midges, and they shuddered; 'Awful' they said.

We set off along a well–defined stalking track, leaving the stream after a while to climb in zig–zags to Mam Selig, the bealach leading to the Loyne valley. The direct route along the old road which goes due north from Tomdoun was drowned when the Loyne was dammed at its northern end. Hamish Brown in his account of walking across Scotland suggests that in drought conditions the old road across the loch becomes exposed and makes it possible to walk across; the people at Heatherlea had described how they had done this some years ago, but afterwards had been alarmed when told by an engineer friend of the likelihood of one of the two bridges, built across deep gorges, collapsing without warning. It had been a very dry few weeks, but we opted for the safe way, aimimg to cross the Loyne river upstream of the loch.

It started to rain, just an advance warning, as we descended from the bealach, and crossed swampy ground to the river. I had heard all sorts of horror stories about the Loyne crossing, but with river and loch very low we were able to walk across, making the occasion something of an anti–climax; boulder-hopping is not one of my skills, but there is a certain satisfaction to be gained from negotiating one of these natural barriers.

We climbed the opposite hillside a little way and found the path leading down the valley to an old ruin, where, in a temporary lull, we sat and ate the substantial sandwiches provided by the hotel. There was then five hundred feet of climbing to reach the old road, rising from its temporary immersion.

We reached the road just as the rain started in earnest, the first real rain since Kershope Bridge. I don't count the occasional thundery shower. After twenty–seven days of settled weather this was the change to unsettled conditions which was going to continue for the rest of the walk. I wasn't too sorry about it cooling off; I realised how much I had been affected by the heat of the past few days, but hoped that the rain would know when to stop.

Today it was obviously setting in, a good Scottish downpour, with the hills gradually fading out. On this good surface there were no route–finding problems, and we descended towards Loch Cluanie, looking across it to the glen which led to Glen Affric and the next stage of the walk. Before starting on this section there was going to be a hiatus off–route at Shiel Bridge where Caroline would be joining me on Monday.

We came to the motor road just short of Cluanie Inn, and finding there was a two–hour wait for the next bus down the glen, thumbed a lift with a woman driver bound for Skye. Hitch–hiking in Scotland tends to be more successful than in over–populated England; drivers are aware that with infrequent or non–existent public transport hitch–hiking can be the only means of getting about for those lacking their own transport. Even so, people tend to be selective about who they offer lifts to and it turned out that our senior citizen status acted in our favour; grey hairs do have some advantages.

It is a long way down Glen Shiel, too far to walk on a wet afternoon; our lift dropped us by the Glenelg turning and we walked up the road to find Shiel House, our weekend's lodging.
June 14th: A wet day, cloud down to the level of the loch; the cyclists staying at Shiel House had had enough of wind and rain after struggling in the teeth of the weather from Inverness and were turning tail for home. Dick had planned for a mountain day, but this wasn't going to be it and we spent the morning getting wet walking round the head of the loch, then retreated to loaf around the house; a good day, perhaps, not to be in a wet tent.

We walked down to Kintail Lodge for an evening meal, then back to watch a gory thriller on TV; I became so involved in the action that I had to shake myself at its end to remember where I was.

June 15th: Dick was up early to catch the bus to Fort William, taking with him every bit of my luggage that I thought I could safely discard. As I stood in the rain watching the bus disappear up the road I was suddenly overwhelmed with homesickness, a longing to be safely back home if only for a few hours. The future seemed hazardous and uncertain and I felt feeble and ill-equipped to tackle the next demanding sections of the walk.

In the early afternoon Caroline drove up from a working week-end in the Lake District, and the enterprise immediately shifted into another gear. Caroline had brought along tent and a lot of food and we spent a busy afternoon sorting out kit, then went to the shop around the corner to buy last-minute provisions. In the face of Caroline's optimism I began to feel better, and to believe that I might indeed be capable of reaching Cape Wrath, which was now about a hundred and fifty miles distant.

Kinlochewe

A 832

Loch a' Chroisg

Achnasheen

A 896

Loch Clair

Loch Coulin

Gerry's Hostel

Craig

A 890

Loch Calavie

Glen Elchaig

Glen Affric

Cluanie Inn

To Shiel Bridge

A 87

Loch Cluanie

14: Of Drumlins and Desperation.

Tuesday June 16th: I was dismayed at the increased weight of my pack after loading up with provisions for ten days, but Caroline cheerfully took on the role of Sherpa, adding tent and cooking stove to her pile. We said good–bye to Mrs Campbell, and drove back to Cluanie. At the hotel we talked to the friendly barman, who said 'Ye're crazy' on learning of our plans, but agreed to let us leave the car safely outside the hotel for Caroline to collect at the end of her stint. It felt decisive to be starting up Glen nan Chaorann. Caroline said, 'We'll take this really slowly,' and set off looking confident and capable.

Caroline, like her three brothers, shares our love of the countryside, and has made outdoor activities her career, her job often involving taking parties on expeditions into the hills. She relishes being in wild and lonely places, and was looking forward to being in an area of Scotland she had not previously visited. As for me I knew I would appreciate a rare opportunity of spending time with my daughter as well as gaining reassurance in the knowledge of her skills in routefinding and mountain survival techniques.

There's a way many hill tracks over passes in Scotland have of starting as clear and well–graded, gradually becoming less broad and smooth, and finally disappearing altogether in the boggy ground of watersheds, where the passage of feet makes little impression; so we weren't disappointed when even this highway into Glen Affric became less well defined. It's reassuring that no one has as yet succeeded in bulldozing a track into this beautiful glen.

High hills began to enfold us as we ascended gently: to our left the shapely peak of Ciste Dhubh, to our right the craggy slopes of Mullach Fraioch Choire. We reached the bealach, and

across Glen Affric was Sgurr nan Ceathreamhnan of the unpro-
nounceable name flanking the glen where we would be walking
tomorrow. We left the course of the stream and traversed the
hillside, to come within sight of the red roofs of Allt Beithe, the
most remote Scottish youth hostel, only accessible on foot or
with difficulty by bicycle.

On the descent to the river I had a spectacular tumble;
unaccustomed as yet to a heavier pack I tripped and couldn't save
myself, so landed with my head and shoulders in a peaty pool.
Caroline was alarmed but the only damage suffered was to my
dignity. We crossed the bridge to the hostel buildings.

Lying on the grassy sward outside the closed door were two
young women, sheltering in sleeping–bags from the chilly breeze.
We discovered them to be German, who had walked in from
Cannich, a long walk of more then twenty miles. A handwritten
notice on the door pronounced the hostel closed until five p.m,
which surprised me in this remote spot. It wasn't until we had
made tea on our Trangia stove, and five o'clock had come and
gone that we thought of trying the door, which was, of course
open. Feeling rather foolish we settled in. Just as well, since it
turned out that the warden had walked to Cannich on his weekly
shopping expedition and was unlikely to be back for some hours.

The hostel began to fill up with an all–male complement; as far
as I could tell, they were all Munro–baggers, who are to be
found in abundance in this region of high mountains.

Munro–bagging, the ascent of all of the two hundred and
seventy–seven Scottish peaks with a height of over three
thousand feet, is a game any reasonably fit and competent walker
can play, but it needs a special kind of dedication to identify and
reach all the named hills. Some of these are in the most remote
areas of Scotland, needing long approach marches. Many involve
rock scrambles, and one, the Inaccessible Pinnacle of Sgurr
Dearg on the island of Skye needs a rope.

The conversion of the Ordnance Survey to the metric system,
has, I've always thought, made life difficult for Munro–baggers
in justifying their obsession. It doesn't have quite the same ring
to say I'm planning to climb all the mountains in Scotland more
than nine hundred and fourteen point four metres high. Perhaps

166

future map–makers will devise some way of identifying Munros, just as they do long–distance trails, to make things easier for Munro–baggers.

I have never had any strong inclination to collect all the Munros, but can boast having stood on the summits of: two of the most remote, Seana Braigh and Lurg Mor; the most northerly, Ben Hope; the most inaccessible, the Pinnacle of that name; and the highest, Ben Nevis. Perhaps before I get much older I should try to add the most southerly, Ben Lomond.

The Munro–baggers at Glen Affric were all, it seemed, aloof Englishmen with penetrating middle–class voices, the kind that are capable of cowing fourteen–year–old youths in the class–rooms of independent schools. These residents seemed to have little time to spare for those just making their way through the area rather than standing on its summits. So we didn't have much to say to one another. It wasn't exactly the kind of friendly talk–ative evening I'd come to expect in places where walkers meet.

June 17th: The warden had returned in the small hours having walked thirty miles or more, although he professed not to be a hill–climber. We paid a modest overnight fee, did rudimentary cleaning tasks, received a coveted stamp on our SYHA membership cards and set off up the glen.

The clearance of yesterday had gone, and it was a grey morning, with the wind in the west and clouds low on the hills. We soon turned away from the main track on to the stalker's path up Gleann Gnomhaidh. Spatters of rain greeted us, blown in the gusty wind. About a mile up the path we met two young people, French, we thought, who asked us the way to the waterfall – the Falls of Glomach, a local Mecca for visitors. The falls plunge down a precipitous hillside into Glen Elchaig some miles to the north. To reach them requires a long walk over rough ground.

We realised that our questioners had gone badly astray, and since they lacked map or compass directed them back to their campsite near Loch Duich by a easier route.

The good path took us into low cloud and mist at Loch a Bealach, where it turned to climb to Bealach an Sgairne and another route back to Morvich. There should have been a path going our way, but if it existed we failed to find it, and were soon crossing drumlins and threading our way through peat hags, trying to find the best way through this wild landscape, with the wind blowing cold. I put on woolly hat and gloves, hardly believing that a few days ago I had been trying to keep cool.

In this difficult country it took us a long time to cover a few miles; we were aiming for Glen Elchaig, where a track came in from Glen Carron, another highway into the hills. From there we would head for the motor road at Achnashellach, still more than a day's march away. We came out of the cloud and into views of more hills, a glen leading down to Falls of Glomach, and our own path disappearing down a steep hillside.

I had been this way before, from the opposite direction, so knew the way down to be steep, descending grassy slopes above a rocky gorge and waterfall, but the path seemed to have deteriorated badly, blocked by a landslide in one place, and descending a forty–five–degree rib. I am less secure in exposed places than I used to be, and had a bad few minutes wondering what would happen if I slipped, until we reached a shallow gully and picked our way to its foot.

We paused on a flat grassy shelf feeling rather pale, me from sheer quaking terror, Caroline from the effort of sustaining my courage; we looked around us. A few feet below was the river, subsiding after its turbulent passage from the waterfall, and flowing calmly between rocky banks to where it did another leap towards the floor of the glen another hundred meters below us. Across the river rose craggy hills, and a rocky gully with mountain ash clinging to its side. Down a subsidiary glen a few feet below we could see the easier path we might have taken descending by a deer fence. The mist and murk had given way to patches of blue. As a campsite it was too good to leave behind and it didn't take long for us to decide that here we would spend the night.

I made the tea while Caroline pitched the tent, one of the modern kind with hoops instead of poles; the last time I had slept in a mountain tent it had a been a World War Two bivvy, and this was luxury, with an inner tent designed to keep out the midges, and a strong outer flysheet which looked capable of withstanding whatever Scottish weather could throw at it. We settled in and relaxed, then found to our horror that somewhere along the way Caroline had lost her new Therm–a–rest sleeping mat! We abandoned any notion of going back to look for it, deciding that in this trackless country we might search unsuccessfully for hours; perhaps some future backpacker would have a lucky find.

We prepared and ate oxtail soup, pasta and hot chocolate crunch pudding, washed down by relays of tea and coffee, and turned in early. I lay in my comfortable new softie sleeping bag and drifted into sleep lulled by the gentle wind and sound of runnIng water.

June 18th: We descended the hillside to Carnach, the building we had seen from above, and crossed the river to reach the estate road; it was a fine morning, early mist clearing to blue skies and promising to be hot. The glen, miles from any public road, seemed unnaturally civilised, with telephone wires to the house, and a tractor working in a field by the river. There were sheep about, and placid shaggy–coated Highland cattle. These are not nearly as fearsome as their long horns suggest, looking like more–than–life–sized cuddly toys with their gentle faces and huge sad eyes.

We came to the end of the estate road at Iron Lodge, and turned on to the stalking track up the An Crom Allt, a steep thousand–foot climb and hot, so we were glad to stop by the river to cool off after reaching easier ground. The path took us over another watershed, with yet more hills coming into view, and descended gently over boggy ground to turn a corner and reach a red–roofed bothy. This small refuge is virtually surrounded by water and I had memories of paddling across on a previous visit, but somone had made a causeway across the stream outside the bothy and we crossed dry–shod.

We stopped for a brew and sat outside in the sun eating sardines and browsing through the bothy book. Someone should make a collection of things written by bothy users, there's always something of interest to read, of where people have been or are going, or comments on life, the universe and everything as seen through the eyes of hill–lovers.

We walked across the swampy glen to cross the river near the outflow of the loch; this did need a paddle. I make no pretence of trying to keep my feet dry when crossing Scottish rivers, my balance is too uncertain for boulder–hopping, and I would rather have wet boots than wet body and pack; so I usually take off my socks and replace boots to walk across, which is perfectly safe unless the water is very high. Scottish rivers can be hazardous after very heavy rain and it is always worth choosing a route carefully with this in mind. This year, however, despite a wet spring there were no real problems with river crossings.

There was a trackless section to follow, a traverse along the lower slopes of the opposite hillside, drumlins and peathags in profusion, with bogwood everywhere, revealed by the dry weather. Bogwood is the remnants of old forests, trees thousands of years old embedded in the peat, fantastic gaunt unearthly shapes arising from the ground like horns and heads of prehistoric animals. Caroline was in her element here, seeming to have an unerring eye in finding the best way through the contorted mass of obstacles.

This is wonderful country, in the midst of remote peaks, wave upon wave of high hills accessible only to people prepared to walk miles for their summits. We came round the hillside to see Lurg Mor and Bidean a Choire Sheisgaich, two of the remoter Munros. With Dick and two sons I had climbed Lurg Mor ten years ago, descending to Patt Lodge, with a six–mile walk along Loch Monar to bring us back to the bothy.

We crossed the glen and another river and came to the path which descends to Loch Calavie and Bendronaig Lodge. On its far side were the ruins of a shieling and another grassy spot just large enough for a tent. With some fishy–looking clouds around, and the weather closing in it was time to camp.

I woke sometime in the small hours to hear spatters of rain and another sound, a recurrent pig–like snuffling and grunting coming from not very far away. I lay awake for a while wondering if I should be worried, then woke Caroline to listen, and we speculated about its source; could it be the Grey Man of Lurg Mor, a brown bear, or an escaped haggis, we wondered. It was none of these, of course; in the morning we saw a hind and her calf grazing peacefully not far above us on the hillside.

170

June 19th: We wandered along the gravelly shores of Loch Calavie, glassy–smooth on a calm morning, the path becoming more pronounced with signs of attempts to promote vehicle access as we climbed to a watershed. Where the track turned west to go to Bendronaig Lodge we took a stalker's path around the lower slopes of Bidein a Choire Sheasgaich. This was a boon to loaded backpackers, threading its way unerringly across stony hillsides to deposit us high on the slopes of Beinn Tharsuinn above the Bearness river. From here there was an hour's rough going to Bealach Bearness at six hundred and fifty metres, over two thousand feet.

This was spectacular country, with more high hills appearing; the peat hags had gone and we scrambled across scree–covered hillsides alive with deer, they just scampering away at our approach. It was a hot climb and the V of the bealach took a long time to come closer.

We had seen no–one since leaving the camping spot above Glen Elchaig so once over the bealach it was strange to find a well–used path and people, first four young women on a Duke of Edinburgh award scheme, followed by a party of half a dozen youngsters, then two older men, who said that they were taking part in the Boots across Scotland day, which was planned for Sunday, the summer solstice, I realised with a shock. Boots across Scotland aims to have a climber on every Munro summit, with sponsorship proceeds going to climbing charities.

The little flurry of traffic subsided as we descended to the foot of the bealach and crossed the river to a grassy spot where we stopped to brew up. This would have been a good place to camp but we opted instead for a bed at Gerry's hostel, so continued along the track, a long walk with more climbing to do before descending through Forestry Commission land. As we went we talked about the next stage of the journey from Kinlochewe, which would involve crossing the wilderness through the Fisherfield Forest. It was an exciting prospect, and a daunting one with the weather less than settled, but Caroline was sure by now that we would succeed, with the psychological advantage of having completed the rough stuff from Cluanie.

We crossed the railway line into the main road, and found

Gerry's Hostel just around the corner, with welcome signs hung out. There was nobody much about, just a walker we had last seen at the foot of the bealach, and a German woman who was touring Scotland. There were civilised things like beds, and a rather temperamental shower.

In the common–room the first thing I noticed was the stuffed fox hanging from the ceiling. Like other objects in the room it looked as if it had been there a long time; its coat had faded to a dull brownish–grey from what had been a red fox pelt; but it looked somehow alive, legs extended as if streaking for its lair.

It was a high ceiling and there were other things hanging from it, bits of mountain–side and stuffed birds and these somehow set the scene for the whole of Gerry's Hostel. The room was large; two shabby comfortable settees faced each other framing a fireplace holding the remnants of a wood fire. A stern notice above one settee proscribed smoking on pain of expulsion, and another reserved a space for Gerry.

One wall was covered with books and periodicals of all kinds, another held hundreds of twelve–inch records, and loudspeakers and hi–fi equipment were draped around the remaining wall-space.

Gerry's Hostel is by way of being an institution for climbers and walkers, placed on the road which gives access on its north side to the Coulin Pass leading to the mighty hills of Torridon. To the south is the wilderness country we had just walked through, with the next road a good day's walk away.

Gerry was out, we learned; little events like the advent of a hostel–full of weekend mountaineers weren't going to interrupt his social evening in Achnasheen. But the food store was open, you took what you wanted and paid later. After a diet of dehydrated food we were spoilt for choice as to what to eat for supper; in the end we settled for Irish stew, a tin each supplemented by a tin of carrots, followed that with peaches with rice pudding and gluttonously ate the whole of a packet of chocolate digestive biscuits.

In June it never really gets dark in north Scotland, so the evenings get extended, and it was already late when a party from Aberdeen arrived, and brought in with them the midges.

Midges are the plague of Scotland that doesn't get mentioned in the brochures; to walk through a swarm of them is like being stroked by a million tiny insistent fingers. If someone were to invent such a torture Amnesty would immediately cry foul.

Midges can drive otherwise sane and reliable people to desperation; I remember being beset when camping with the family in Glen Torridon. Dick disappeared up the mountainside to eat his breakfast porridge on a high ledge and Robert, our youngest, retired to his sleeping bag for the day and refused to get up. When midges swarm the best thing to do is to stay indoors and try to keep them out. So I was amazed when Caroline said she was going for a walk.

It was a warm windless evening, just the weather midges like best, but Caroline enveloped herself from head to foot in jeans and anorak and wound a scarf around head and face so that only her eyes showed, as if she were in a desert sandstorm. The rest of us stayed in the common–room, Gerry's effortlessly having absorbed what seemed a large number of people.

The walker whom we had last seen on the way down several hours ago came and talked about his most recent collection of Munros, telling me that there were seven of these mountains in the hills we had just crossed. He had passed the two hundred mark and was on the home straight and had taken the opportunity afforded by being made redundant in the winter to put all his energies into the Munros; he had, he said, done forty this year. My own disclosure that I was walking to Cape Wrath was passed over as being only slightly less boring than, say, an enthusiasm for collecting used Mars bar wrappers, since there aren't any Munros at Cape Wrath.

The telephone had been ringing on and off all evening and in Gerry's absence no one had taken the responsibility of answering it. It rang again as I was passing on my way to make cocoa so I picked it up and without waiting for the caller to speak said that Gerry was out and could they phone again.

The voice at the other end said, 'This is Gerry', so we continued from there.

Gerry asked me to find out how many of the Ptarmigan Club from Aberdeen had arrived, and while I was doing this the line seemed to have been disconnected so I put the receiver down and went on making the cocoa. It rang again, and this time Caroline, coming in from her close encounter with the midges, answered it. There ensued quite a long conversation, and at the end of it Caroline came into the common-room looking somewhat put out.

It turned out that the exchange with Gerry had been less than friendly, although I couldn't quite understand why, only that Gerry wanted a lift back from Achnasheen. One of the people with transport saw to that, and we were safely in bed before Gerry returned.

June 20th: As I descended the staircase the next morning the first words I heard were those of the Munro-man, saying that he'd done forty this year. It was after this that I discovered he was talking to Gerry so I thought I'd better introduce myself. As often happens after an unfortunate beginning, we found that we liked each other. We declared a truce, and Gerry produced for breakfast the goodies we'd been missing during our sojourn in the wilderness, bananas and apples and luscious yoghurt and real bread.

Everybody else had left early, but we stayed around talking, philosophising, taking photographs, and waving to the driver of the train that ran along the end of the garden. This was a real oasis in the walk and we tore ourselves away reluctantly, with farewell kisses from Gerry.

The track proper over the Coulin Pass starts at Achnashellach but Gerry had told us about a footpath just up the road which would cut off a corner and avoid two miles of road-walking. The path, marked by an almost illegible signpost started at a place where a steep cutting had been made in some road-works. I balked at the prospect of heaving myself up the precipitous bank and had to be coaxed by Caroline, who has a rooted objection to walking on roads. Once safely over the fence, however, it was a good wee path, heading unerringly uphill in zig-zags through the trees and coming out at the top of a fire-break just above the point where the main track does a hair-pin bend.

I learned later that this was an old stalker's path which had fallen into disuse, but had recently been restored and cleared by, among others, Hamish Brown, a real boon to people walking

174

north from Craig.

This was the easiest walking since the military road near Cluanie, and we found we'd almost crossed our second map together. Caroline pointed out that I was now less than three maps' distance away from Cape Wrath, which I still couldn't quite grasp as being within reach. There should have been good views of the Torridon hills but these were obscured in cool cloud. The miles went by quickly and we descended to Torran-Coulin and sat by the river to eat sardines and the last of Gerry's bread. Another stage of the walk would soon be coming to an end, as sherpa Caroline would be leaving me at Dundonnell to head for home in Nottingham, and we had to think about ways and means for her return to Cluanie to recover her car.

Of the two possible routes to Kinlochewe I chose what looked the easier, a track through the forest to Coulin Lodge. Caroline wanted to take the path over the hill to avoid any road–walking; so we separated for the afternoon, arranging to meet in Kinlochewe. I descended to Coulin Lodge and Loch Clair, noting that walkers were carefully routed outside the forest fence. There were drifts of water–lilies on the calm water, the rhododendrons giving way to foxgloves and purple ling, a reminder that the year would be on the turn after tomorrow's solstice. Nearer the road I found a clump of small white orchids, a prosaic name for beautiful flowers.

The bulk of Beinn Eighe began to dominate the forward view. What memories of a lifetime these mountains hold; an October honeymoon visit when we traversed Liathach, descending in the dark to the road at the head of the glen; family holidays with the children at the Torridon estate cottages, Stables and Balgy. Here the children had learned their mountain–craft on Torridon's hills, had swum in its lochs and fished in its rivers. Torridon for me meant so much more than just the mountains, and to be here had a home–coming feeling.

I came to the main road and trudged the two miles downhill to Kinlochewe. Caroline was nowhere to be seen, although in mileage she had a shorter distance to cover, but I guessed that her route might have been less than straightforward. I looked around for B&B signs, and soon found Mrs Corlett at Slioch

Terrace, a little row of houses off the main road opposite the hotel. Caroline appeared while I was in the bath, Mrs Corlett having spotted her walking into town, and guessed who she was. Caroline had had a strenuous afternoon's walk; one section of the old path she took had been planted over, so she had had to fight her way through spruce forest, and was feeling somewhat the worse for wear.

We went across to the hotel for a meal, and then telephoned Dick, who was flung into a panic when we suggested he drive to meet us in Dundonnell the following Wednesday; hardly surprising, since he had been home for less than a week after his trip to Fort William and would need to leave early on Tuesday for the rendezvous. Dick was sure that what we were asking was impossible and we had to use all our persuasive powers to convince him that he could do all his preparation and leave London within forty-eight hours.

June 21st: Rest day; tension relaxed after the efforts of the last five days, I had to drag myself out of bed to a magnificent breakfast with good Scottish porridge to start. On a grey drizzly morning we weren't tempted towards the hills, but wandered down the road to buy Sunday paper and goodies at the petrol station. We went to look at the visitor centre, full of excellently presented material relating to the area, geology, botany and wild life all being covered. There were bright pictures of the dragonflies of which we had seen at least three species, iridescent green, turquoise, and with wasp-like stripes. I learned that these only thrive in purest environmental conditions, nice to know these still exist somewhere.

We spent a lazy lunch-hour in the hotel eating toasted sandwiches and reading the Sunday paper, then back to sit outside watching the siskins coming to feed at Mrs Corlett's bird-table. We talked with Mrs Corlett about our plans. Kinlochewe's livelihood is all connected with the hills whether in farming or estate management or tourism, and the local people are well in touch with what goes on in the area. We were intrigued to learn that next weekend Kinlochewe would be the venue for the Three Lochs Challenge, a long distance walk of the kind we were accustomed to doing in less demanding countryside.

We had a fish and chip supper at the hotel, busy with walkers coming back from a day in the hills; at Caroline's recommendation I tried Guinness, which seemed good for me. Caroline said 'I can't wait' [to start tomorrow's trek], I feeling the now common mixture of excitement and apprehension, but becoming increasingly certain that the only uncertainty now was the weather.

Scoraig

Little Loch Broom

Badralloch

Ferry

Loch Broom

Ullapool

Camusnagul

Dundonnell

A 832

A 835

Corrie Hallie

Lochan Fada

Kinlochewe to Ullapool.

Kinlochewe

15: A tent in the wilderness

Monday June 22nd: The weather forecast was good for Wimbledon, less favourable for Wester Ross, which had the only squiggle of a weather front in the UK running across it. The tops were in cloud and the wind blowing cool from the north–west.

Between Kinlochewe and Corrie Hallie near Dundonnell lies another great wilderness, the Letterewe and Fisherfield forests, accessible only on foot, and a jealously guarded game preserve. It is a mere twenty–three map miles across the wilderness from south to north, but this includes a trackless section and some large rivers which can be impassable in spate conditions. You need to be above–average fit to do the crossing in a day, and people wishing to tackle the half–dozen prized Munros in the area have to be prepared to camp or to stay at the only open bothy available outside the stalking season.

Many years earlier I had looked into the wilderness from the summit of Slioch, the magnificent sandstone mountain which dominates Kinlochewe. This was on a memorable family expedition, six of us including a nine–year old. What with the long approach walk alongside Loch Maree and many stops to admire the view it had been a ten–hour day. There was a herd of very smelly goats high on the hillside.

From the summit I looked down on the shining eye of Lochan Fada and beyond to huge unfamiliar hills. Far to the north at the foot of a long valley rose the crenellated towers of another splendid hill which I found later to be An Teallach. It all looked supremely unattainable, a Scottish Shangri–La, and as the years went by it came to seem less likely that I would ever walk into this special hidden country. So I couldn't quite believe that I was actually here and on my way.

From Incheril a Land–Rover track led round the hillside and

followed the river to the Heights of Kinlochewe, where there are a few deserted buildings. Two women with a dog walking ahead turned right up a side valley while we turned to climb into Gleann na Muice, Caroline grumbling about the 'improved' track. As we came to the spot where the track turned into an indistinct line through soggy vegetation we became engulfed in descending cloud and the rain started, nasty cold driving rain. It wasn't the kind of weather I had envisaged for this part of the walk, and I felt rather cheated as we arrived on the shores of Lochan Fada.

This must be one of the most beautiful spots in Scotland, far from anywhere and surrounded by majestic hills; if you could see them, that is. The water of the loch was whipped into waves by the west wind, with the cloud cover not far above it. We decided we had had enough of the weather and found the perfect campsite by the loch shore, a green sward which must have been idyllic given the right conditions. It was a spot for basking in the sun, not huddling in a tent.

Caroline gave me a lesson in pitching her tent, which she was entrusting to me and Dick for the next section of the walk. We brewed up and had extra-late lunch and, thoroughly chilled, I crawled into my sleeping bag to warm up. After a while the rain moderated and Caroline went off to reconnoitre the next section of the route, which would be trackless and would take us over Bealach na Croise.

It was just a temporary lull and Caroline came back after an hour thoroughly wetted but having succeeded in spotting the bealach through the murk. We spent what remained of the day reading. I finished *The Woman in White* and swapped it with Caroline for *The Looking-Glass War*, hoping that the weather would improve before we had run out of reading matter, one of my worst fears. I remember the acute boredom of spending an Easter weekend in a French hotel in Brittany, Dick and I both laid low with 'flu, having finished everything we had brought to read, and being reduced to watching bad French TV

June 23rd: At about 5.00am the wind dropped; I peeped out of the tent to see cloud lying on the water and went back to sleep. An hour or so later the wind started up again and brought with it more driving rain from the north-west. We stayed rather dis-

180

consolately in the tent, and I started to worry; tomorrow we were to meet Dick in Dundonnell, which was still two bealachs distant.

I couldn't help seeing an awesome majesty in the weather, with the clouds swirling round great hidden hills, and waters of the loch lashed into spray in the fierce wind but I didn't fancy being out in it. We were just a half–day's walk from Kinlochewe, but I felt vulnerable in being stranded in a mountain tent. Caroline was shocked by my pessimism, seeing the weather just as an acceptable aspect of any expedition.

At about twelve–thirty there seemed to be something of a lull; not exactly your ideal conditions but at least we could see something. Caroline's tent has the advantage that all the packing can be done in the dry inside the outer flysheet so we weren't forced to expose ourselves to the elements until the last minute, when we were geared up in cagoules. Caroline looked at me and said 'Shall we go for it?' and off we went.

We climbed up the hillside to a moraine ridge overlooking the little lochan which Caroline had recced the previous day. From here we were able to see the bealach, a true V–shaped breche. There followed a mile or so of rough going to descend to the Tana–gaidh river flowing out of Coire Mhic Fhearchair. There were some splendid falls cascading down a series of rocky shelves, the sort of thing which would have attracted crowds anywhere near a road. We went higher to cross the river, swollen by the rain, and from there climbed a stony hillside to the bealach.

The weather looked better on the other side; the rain had stopped and through the veil of lifting clouds we could see to the north the shape of An Teallach standing sentinel above the glen. Just fifty feet below the bealach we found the beginnings of a path not marked on the map, which improved as we descended. It was soon dry enough for a brief halt for late lunch.

We came down to the glen floor past hillsides clad in shining white quartzite as if overlaid with mother–of–pearl; below us was Loch an Nid, where we joined another stalker's path coming in from the Destitution Road near Braemore junction past Loch a Bhraoin. This felt more familiar; just a few miles in that direction was the way into Nest of Fannich, where Dick and I had spent idyllic days in what I have always thought of as our vintage Scottish year, 1982.

We had visited Nest of Fannich after a memorable few days in Gleann Beag when we had 'done' all the Deargs, the lovely group of hills above the Inverlael Forest. At the Glenbeg bothy we had met Nancy Smith, staying there with her young grandson and similarly engaged in climbing mountains. It was Nancy who told us about Nest of Fannich and other delectable hidden corners of Scotland, learned about in a lifetime's wandering from her base at Fersit. I was immensely saddened to read last year of Nancy's sudden death, and the news later of Nest of Fannich's destruction by fire seemed to set a seal on one time of my life.

We walked alongside Loch an Nid and descended steeply to reach the river below more waterfalls. We paddled across to a flowery meadow where we pitched the tent for what was to be Caroline's last night in the wilderness. The brief clearance was soon over, and all night the wind blew strongly from the south, heralding yet another kink in the weather front.

June 24th: Expecting more rain, we were up and away earlier, with the clouds steadily descending to pursue us down the glen. We came to the place where the river turns to Strath na Sealga and Shenavall, and stopped for a breather by the ruins of a croft, now no more than a pile of stones. This green place between two rivers protected by its bastion of high hills was heartachingly beautiful and at the same time unimaginably desolate as if its long–gone inhabitants had left in these sad stones traces of their own pain and loss in what once must have been a self–sufficient community.

We followed the steep track out of the glen with the slopes of An Teallach above us now wreathed in wet cloud, climbing again to the thousand–foot contour on to moorland scattered with small plates of water. The rain began in earnest as we descended the track into Gleann Chaorochain, now meeting the occasional walker.

Corrie Hallie was the end of the walk for Caroline, who was heading south tomorrow for Nottingham and work. As a beginning we were going off–route here for Dundonnell so we stood by the roadside to hitch a lift. Cars were hurtling by without any sign of wanting to stop for wet walkers, so we were relieved to see after a half–hour the familiar sight of our yellow VW motor caravan. It was still only early afternoon and I'd warned Dick not to expect us until five o'clock time, so in his surprise he nearly failed to stop.

It was getting late for lunch but Caroline and I insisted that we must have a drink to celebrate the successful conclusion of an important stage of the walk, so we parked outside the Dundonnell Hotel and went into the bar, to be greeted unexpectedly by Charlie Rose, with his wife Priscilla. We had first met Charlie many years ago in London, as members of a group of climbers who used to meet regularly at the Tivoli Hotel in the Strand, this demolished many years ago. Charlie and Priscilla now own a guesthouse in Inveralligan near Torridon, and were having a day off from their duties and doing some sight–seeing of their own. It was one of those happy coincidences to meet here, so we spent a pleasant hour exchanging news and gossip.

By now Caroline and I were feeling it had been a long time since breakfast, so we drove a half–mile down the road to park in a lay–by by the side of Little Loch Broom. I had last been here in 1989, when I had spent a lazy afternoon reading and writing while waiting for Dick who was fulfilling a long–held ambition of doing the traverse of An Teallach. Today was not mountain weather, with the cloud down to the loch and the soft rain falling steadily, but it was still a perfect spot. Dick had brought all sorts of goodies from home, so we, starved of real food, ate gluttonously of home–baked bread and home–grown salad followed by raspberries and cream, and revelled at being for a while at least under cover, and at the successful conclusion to a vital section of the walk.

Hunger satisfied at last we drove down the road to Camusnagul and Mrs Duncan's house by the lochside, a comfortable sanctuary after spartan nights in a tent. Like many of the landladies we met Mrs Duncan knew all about long–distance walking and regaled us with stories of other walking parties who had passed through her doors. It was here that I was to say good–bye to my dear faithful Sherpa, so we had a long sorting–out session in preparation for the final stages of the walk, when I would have

Dick 's company. Cape Wrath still felt a long way distant but each stage completed was making it seem more likely that I was actually going to reach it.

16: A talent for improvisation

Thursday June 25th: We left on a perfect Scottish morning. What a wonderful interlude this had been, bringing together two of my nearest and dearest, good food and company, the best Scottish hospitality, and a surprise meeting to add spice to the occasion.

We drove back to Corrie Hallie where I disembarked, leaving Dick to drive Caroline to Cluanie to retrieve her car. I set off along the minor road towards Badralloch with a light pack, having left most of my gear to be carried in the VW. After the rain the hills and loch were sparklingly clear and the air fresh; every ridge and gully of An Teallach was sharply defined and I kept stopping to look. I climbed steadily through larch forest then across black peaty moorland with sheep wandering across the unfenced road. At its summit the road turns sharply to head for Badralloch and the Scoraig peninsula; this corner of Ross–shire, once depopulated, has been recolonised by incomers.

I went forward towards Allt na Airbhe, a tiny settlement with access only by the rough track I was taking, or by water across the loch from Ullapool, but with a renowned gourmet hotel. I came to a tiny shining lochan, becoming excited as the view unfolded of the white houses of Ullapool with their backing of familiar hills. Behind the flat spit of land which houses the town rises a wedge–shaped steep–sided hill, not a high one, but unmistakable in silhouette, and seen from afar as an identifying feature of Ullapool. I sat beside the lochan for a breather and began to wonder where the midges were; this was real midge country with water for breeding and heather to hide in, but wherever the midges were they weren't here.

I descended a hillside scarred with a new Land–rover track,

North
Sea

A838
Gualin House

Strath Dionard

Glen Golly

Lochinver

A838 Overscaig
Hotel

Loch Shin

Maovally

Glen
Cassley

Lairg

Oykel Bridge

Rosehall

Loch an
Daimh

Ullapool

which debouched straight on to the stony loch shore. There was nothing to show that the smart white house with garden chairs on its shaven front lawn was an hotel, but there was a motor–launch drawn up at the jetty and a uniformed man–servant was carrying in cases of foil–topped bottles and boxes of exotic fruit and vegetables. I realised that this was not the kind of place likely to serve bar lunches, but here at least was my ferry across the loch.

With almost an hour to wait I sat by the jetty. It hadn't been easy to find out about the ferry; people at Dundonnell and at the number I had telephoned had seemed reluctant to commit them–selves, but I had been informed that 'there should be a ferry at about two'. It was reassuring to see the boat actually there but I wasn't going to risk letting it get away without me. The wind blew sharp and cool from the north and ducks ranged freely around the lochside, seeming without fear of humans.

The trip across the loch had the feeling of a sea crossing in choppy waters on the rising tide. I looked south–east to the head of the loch to where the cone shape of Sgurr Mor, the high point of the Fannich range, dominated the view and hugged myself in delight that I was so far north.

Ullapool gives the impression of a frontier town, in fact the foreign factory ships which help the town's livelihood in winter have been called Klondykers. From Ullapool north the land becomes progressively more remote and less populated, and the settlements fewer and smaller, so the town tends to be a focus of activity for shopping and business in general. I had been here on other occasions and liked Ullapool, contained within a small space, and with shops and accommodation in plenty. Today the town was quiet, with fishing and leisure craft moored unused in the bay and people from a coach party wandering along the harbour road.

I bought the *Guardian* and went into the Frigate cafe for coffee and a roll, then retired to the little waterfront gardens to read and wait for Dick. There was a good view of the road winding to the top of the hill in the direction from which the car would appear, but I became distracted watching the McBraynes ferry docking from Stornoway and Dick didn't see me as he drove into town, so I spent a strenuous few minutes chasing the car, stick, boots, rucksack and all, until we caught up with each other outside the supermarket.

June 26th: It would have been good to have set off straight away on this the final stage of the walk, but we needed time to replenish supplies and reorganise generally, a recurrent chore on my journey. Next morning we shopped and paid a visit to the tourist information centre with the purpose of securing our getaway from Cape Wrath after our arrival there. We weren't particularly reassured by what we learned: there certainly was transport from Cape Wrath by minibus and ferry to the nearest village of Durness, only subject to the vagaries of wind and weather, and to demand from the mainly tourist clientele. Once at Durness it was a different matter; it seems that all public transport in the north centres on the nearest railhead, Lairg in this instance, and that is where the post–bus went. Lairg is no closer to Ullapool than is Durness.

It was academic really; I was going to Cape Wrath and would find a way back somehow. As for knowing how that might be I was in no worst case than at Newcastleton; just closer that was all. I decided to forget about getting back and to direct all my energies towards getting there.

Feeling that we were burning our boats we drove the thirty–six miles to Rosehall in Strath Oykell to commit ourselves to B&B at Invercassley Cottage for Sunday night and to leave a cache of tent and supplies. The rain came on as we drove back, more of the soft Scottish rain which blotted out hills and coastline alike. The weather seemed to have become established in its summer Scottish mode of one fine day in three, and I could only hope that the fine days would come when most needed. Still and all, I could now count the miles to Cape Wrath; under a hundred to go. The last pieces of the jigsaw were in my hands, ready to be fitted into place. I discarded yet another map, leaving just three to be carried.

June 27th: From Ullapool unless you want to walk along the main road or to climb some large rough mountains there are two possible lines of approach to Cape Wrath; one of these follows the west coast via Achiniver, Ardmore and Kinlochbervie to Sandwood Bay. I have no great liking for coastal walks, and

188

wanted to continue in a direct line up the centre of Scotland. For the next few miles this would entail going generally in a south-easterly direction, such is the complexity of the lie of the land. Like that 'untravelled margin of the world which fades from sight forever and forever as I move' Cape Wrath was receding from me to the north-west.

The VW was left parked safely behind Glendhu where we had spent the night, and we left Ullapool by a rough road along the side of the Ullapool river, through some dusty quarry workings. The track went along the rim of a huge excavation like a giant's teacup then mercifully left these scars behind to cross the river and lead us along a lochside. The terrain had changed; gone were the steep-sided glens and craggy slopes of the Fisherfield Forest, replaced by smoother lower hills and heather moors. We were entering fishing country.

We climbed to a low watershed, and looked back to see the Ullapool hills and beyond them to the unmistakable V-shape of Glen Sligachan cutting through the Cuillin hills of Skye. To the south appeared another familiar shape, of Seana Braigh, a hill laying claim to being the most remote Munro. In those halcyon days of 1982 Dick and I had climbed Seana Braigh from Glen Beag, descending a hillside swarming with deer, to a tiny and remote bothy by a loch. In heatwave conditions we had swum in its calm waters and sunbathed by its side. In three days' walking we had only the company of the deer, and saw no other people.

Another bothy at the far end of Loch an Daimh, was our destination for the night; this small shelter, with no high mountains immediately accessible, seems to have visits mostly from people passing through. I read in the bothy book of one party, like myself bound for Cape Wrath, but taking a different route after Strath Oykel, our next stage. Thank goodness that there is no one traditional End-to-End route.

June 28th: By lunchtime we had reached Oykel Bridge, an easy nine miles along the track, descending to cross the river at Duag Bridge, then through forest to emerge on the main A837 road in Strath Oykel. The afternoon's walk looked easy, along the river, but wasn't, the map failing to show vital bridges, and at one point stranding us on the wrong side of the river. This was a terrain

d to the pursuit of the salmon, with small fishermen's huts
.tervals, beside a wide deeply flowing river, with salmon
.ping, but not a fisherman to be seen. We extricated ourselves
.nd reached a farm track and a little road which forsook the
riverbank for the hillside in a series of roller–coaster swoops. We
could see below the flat alluvial plain and the bridge where we
would rejoin the main road, but in worsening weather it seemed
a long time coming.

We reached Invercassley cottage just in advance of the rain,
with the No Vacancies sign out and were glad we'd booked
ahead. Invercassley was a nice place, comfortable and homely,
with free–range ducks and hens roaming around the garden and
an elderly spaniel snoozing in a corner of the dining–room. Our
fellow guests being car–borne tourists with smaller appetites we
had the best of the good home–cooked food, salmon and fresh
vegetables, and did justice to the generous supply of apple juice.
The mountain photographs in our bedroom were by Ginger Cain,
an old acquaintance from days in Skye, now running a successful
art business in Llanberis.

It had been a hard day, but we were a quarter of the way to
Cape Wrath from Ullapool and had walked across Map 20.

June 29th: Moments of truth! With tent and more food and fuel
added to our burden we set off up Glen Cassley beside another
salmon river, a smaller one than the Oykel, with frequent fishing
reaches alongside. This was more like it; the way from here on
led relentlessly north–west, heading straight for Strath Shinary
and beyond it Cape Wrath. Spatters of rain greeted us, and the
hills ahead were cloaked in mist; we knew that somewhere up
there was Ben More Assynt but we weren't going to see it today.
There were ten miles of tarmac but almost no traffic along this
dead–end thoroughfare. We came upon a fishing party, clad in
upper–class Barbour wear, with attendant dogs, four–wheel drive
Suzukis and wicker picnic basket with bottles.

The tarmac came to an end at Duchally Lodge, where a gate
bore rude notices telling us that we risked being shot! Repulsed,
we descended to a riverside path which we unblocked at one
point and carried on to join an estate road. Once out of sight of
the lodge we found a place to camp where a small stream

190

splashed down through the rocks and heather to join the main river.

We started to unpack the tent: flysheet...yes; inner tent...yes; poles...yes; pegs ....*Where were the pegs?* we looked at each other in horror; somewhere between Dundonnell and Ullapool the tent–pegs had become separated from the rest of the tent. Wherever they were they weren't here; helplessly we up–ended the tent–bag hoping that the pegs would magically appear.

Pause for recriminations; 'I asked you twice and you said they were there'.. 'I don't see where we can have left them'. Me (woefully) 'You know what this means?' envisaging having to return to Ullapool and start all over again. I was particularly aware of my responsibility to Caroline since this was her tent, and I was the one who knew how to put it up; in some odd way I felt I was letting Caroline down.

Dick is made of sterner stuff, choosing to regard such minor setbacks simply as a challenge presenting an opportunity for him to exercise his talent for improvisation. So, having recovered from our first shock horror we set about erecting the tent using local materials, rocks from the stream and twigs from a rowan tree. The result looked less neat and tidy than on previous occasions, but it would do.

I started to make the tea while Dick went off to look for more twigs. He returned some while later looking rather ruffled. It transpired that the branch of a tree had broken under his hand, catapulting him into the stream; he had a bump on his head and minor bruises elsewhere. We passed a subdued evening, but at least the tent was standing up to some minor buffeting. The only drawback was that the endstops which prevented the poles sinking into the ground had been left behind with the pegs, so throughout the night the tent was gradually subsiding into the heather.

June 30th: The cuckoo which had sung our lullaby provided our reveille in the small hours, and its relentless refrain pursued us as we continued to follow the river, with Dick in the rear; he caught me up to show a coil of fence wire gleaned from the wayside. All we needed now was somehow to cut it into sections for pegs. Ahead power and pipe lines converged on the buildings of Duchally Power Station beside a small holding dam; from here water is pumped miles across country to feed the homes and industry of Ullapool. We reached the private waterworks road, and climbed to fifteen hundred feet high on the shoulder of Maovally, becoming enveloped in thin cloud, with the wind blowing cold from the North–east.

We came over the hill to see the attenuated shape of Loch Shin below; on its far side were the white buildings of the Overscaig Hotel, our destination for the night, still an afternoon's walk away. Far to the north–east we saw a high hill which we decided must be Ben Klibreck above Strath Naver, which we had often driven past on our way north from Lairg to a holiday house near Tongue. This really, at last, was the far north; less than fifty miles to go.

It would have been nice to have had a boat; the road did a weary dog–leg to shoot off into a side valley to Corrie Kinloch before turning to cross a causeway to meet the main road. We huddled in a hollow by the wayside to eat lunch, and were astonished to see a group of four motoryclists appearing down the way we'd come from nowhere. 'I bet they're German,' I said, German motorcyclists being an in–family joke, always turning up in the most unlikely places. (Yes, they were Germans.)

At the road I put my thumb up to the first vehicle, a minibus laden with Lowland Scots and camping equipment; I struggled to understand the broad dialect as we drove the two miles off–route to the Overscaig Hotel. The friendly proprietor was unruffled when Dick asked if he had a small workshop. This proved no problem at all; our piece of wire was taken away and returned later cut into meticulously turned tent–pegs.

We soon had a good fug going in the comfortable bedroom and had a make and mend session. We hung up the wet tent in the bathroom to dry then mended the seam of the inner tent which had come apart. We did intensive bathing and dealing with dirty clothes and I took a tuck in my trousers which were becoming embarrassingly loose. What with drinking tea and looking at the view across the peaceful loch the time passed pleasantly until we went down to the bar to talk to the other couple in residence about Cape Wrath; they'd been there the other day, they said, made it seem no big deal at all.

July 1st: In my route notes I'd written that the day started with six miles of main road 'I'm afraid', but it was one of the north Scottish kinds of main road, single track with passing places, and about one vehicle every five minutes. In two hours we had turned on to the estate road leading over the Bealach nam Meirleach, walking between increasingly craggy slopes, the landscape containing as much water as land, with numerous small pools and lochans fringing the track. Clumps of foxgloves made brilliant splashes of colour against the drab hills.

Once over the bealach, the shape of Ben Hope began to occupy the skyline, with its twin Ben Loyal looking over its shoulder. These two hills are old friends, symbolising for me the far north, appearing repeatedly in views from the road which skirts the north coast. Ben Hope by virtue of its Munro status tends to attract the most attention, but the turrets and crags of Ben Loyal and its rough approach over miles of trackless waste make it a connoiseur's mountain, and during family holidays spent on the north coast we had come to appreciate its wild and rugged landscape. It was wonderful to be approaching these hills on foot. At last I was on the long anticipated final map with the words Cape Wrath printed on its cover.

The track led downhill, and we turned a corner to see the buildings of Gobernuisgach Lodge set by the river below, at the end of its private road. There were signs of habitation in opulent–looking cars parked outside, and we made haste to take a short cut over the hillside to take us out of sight above the steep sides of Glen Golly, an impressive deep ravine. For a while the path stayed high on the hillside, then descended through trees to emerge on to a grassy sward by the river, as flat as a cricket pitch. At its far end the land rose steeply and a ribbon of waterfall fell to join the stream. It was the perfect spot for the night's camp.

We paddled across the river, disturbed a complacent sheep with its lamb, and set up camp in the now calm sunny evening, too cold for midges, the new tent pegs giving us a more workmanlike pitch; we ate macaroni cheese for supper with some melon saved from the Overscaig packed lunch. I watched a red sun sinking behind the hill and with rising excitement thought of it setting for the brief hours of darkness over Cape Wrath, now so close.

July 2nd: We climbed out of the glen on to a flat expanse of moorland. A young man driving a hill buggy went by, weaving his way over the rough ground. We crossed the river and climbed a breathtakingly steep shoulder with a craggy drop to the north; beyond it I looked down a glen with precipitous sides to where it debouched upon an expanse of water. This was Glen Beag and at its end was Loch Eriboll, a sea loch giving way to the waters of the northern sea.

At a dark lochan the path divided, the one branch going over by the south of the mountains Foinaven and Arkle to Lone and Loch Stack; we took the less well-defined path to the north leading to a small rocky summit. To the west rose Foinaven clad in silvery quartzite, its awesome slopes descending to the long reaches of Strath Dionard below us. Far in the distance the river did a right-angled turn; along the hillside above it I knew ran the road from Rhiconich to Durness and at its high point was the solitary building of Gualin House, whose white shape I thought I could just see. It looked deceptively close, so much so that for a while I wondered if we might be there in time to make a dash for a night in Durness.

We picked our way the thousand feet down the hillside to the end of Loch Dionard. Outside a fisherman's hut was a small family party, parents and young son, with their boat drawn up at the lochside. Reservedly we exchanged greetings suspecting that we had little in common except our presence, here, for the moment. Progress along the lochside was slow and wearisome, the path having come to an abrupt end. We paddled the river near the loch's outflow, and gained the new track, an ugly bulldozed monument to wheeled transport.

It wasn't easy finding a campsite, with the weather blowing up and we had to settle for lumpy heather by the river. All night the wind blew from the south-east, roaring down the strath; the inner tent kept lifting off its hooks, and engulfing us in flapping nylon. I lay awake wondering if the weather would relent and give us fair skies for the trek to Cape Wrath, now less than twenty miles away. Just two more pieces in the jigsaw.

July 3rd: I was ready for a breathing–space before embarking on the final push, the interval before the last act, so after climbing the hillside to reach the Durness road we again thumbed the first car to appear. It turned out to be an English family party in a BMW and we talked of Scotland and the attractions of the far north. Durness was smaller than expected, an elongated settlement scattered along the road, with its nucleus the general store opposite the filling station. It was bone–chillingly cold, even the locals complaining about the weather. We booked into the Parkhill Hotel and set about replenishing food stores, washing sweaty socks and eating whatever we could lay our hands on. We did a clear–out of excess gear which we would leave behind for our return, after much deliberation deciding to leave the tent behind.

Finding out about the Cape Wrath Ferry was another matter. We knew that a ferry and minibus took tourists to Cape Wrath, but how would they know if there were people waiting to be brought back? What if there happened to be no tourists on Sunday? And what if the ferry couldn't run because of bad weather? These were questions the people we telephoned didn't seem to want to answer. In desperation we turned to Mrs Mackay, who besides managing the hotel ran the store and petrol station as well. Once Mrs Mackay had heard that I'd walked from Beachy Head she sprang into action. One telephone call settled it; yes, there would be someone to pick us up on our arrival from Sandwood, but would we try to get to Cape Wrath in good time if the weather turned bad?

The dining–room at supper was busy with holiday–makers and a party of geologists. Tomorrow would see the end of the walk and we would be just another couple travelling in Scotland. I wondered how it would feel to be free of the need to keep on walking. I wasn't sure I wanted it to come to an end.

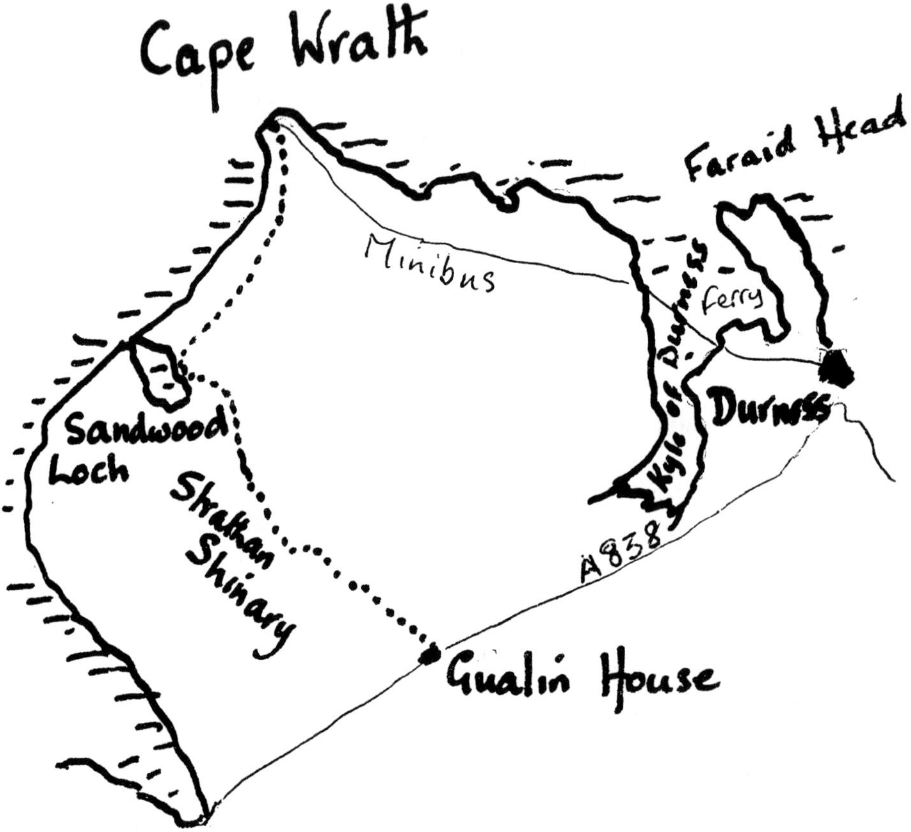

Cape Wrath
Faraid Head
Minibus
Ferry
Kyle of Durness
Durness
Sandwood Loch
Strathan Shinary
A838
Gualin House

17: A peak in Darien

Saturday July 4th: We had an anxious half–hour waiting for a lift outside Durness, 'It only needs one car to stop,' I said. It came eventually, an English couple touring the coast, who said they thought Cape Wrath was 'very pretty'. They set us down at Gualin House just twenty–four hours after we'd left it with the clouds still low over Foinaven but patches of blue appearing.

The route to Strathan and Sandwood crosses a low watershed and from there we made a beeline, along a low ridge covered in sparse brown–tipped grass barely hiding the underlying Torridonian sandstone. Spiky bog asphodel and starry butterwort grew in wet hollows. The landscape replicated in miniature the sterner territory we had encountered earlier, with crags and gullies to negotiate, and a pool or lochan in every dip.

The wind was blowing with an icy breath telling that it came from Arctic snows and the sky had cleared to that inimitable shade of washed–out blue only seen in the far north. As we came over the watershed the view opened out to Strath Shinary. We looked across its far side to craggy slopes; through a gap between two hills was an expanse of open water which I knew stretched past Cape Wrath to the Atlantic, and beyond to America as the first landfall. Along the strath the river wound down to the oval face–shape of Sandwood Loch, topped by the raised eyebrow of Sandwood Bay; the sea, speckled with tiny islands, lapped the crinkled deserted coastline to the west. To the south was a shadowy humped mass pencilled on the horizon which I recognised as Quinag, and, closer, the shapely cone of Ben Stack. It was all impossibly beautiful.

Dick was forging ahead, and I followed slowly, savouring the moment. It was quiet, no sound of bird or beast, only the steady murmur of the wind; I could hear the creak of my rucksack and my own footfall and fancied I could hear my heart beating, while inside me a great feeling of exultation was growing. It wasn't only that I now knew I would reach Cape Wrath, but more about all that had happened to bring me here.

It hadn't been all pleasure, long–distance walking isn't like that. Some of it had been painful, boring, uncomfortable or, frankly, scary, and throughout I had had to wrestle with self–doubt. The conversations with myself which I described in Chapter 2 had frequently been of the 'I can't do it' 'yes you can' variety. So finding myself less than a day's march from Cape Wrath on this perfect day amid this perfect scenery was just overwhelming. The moment had the effect of bringing together all the experiences of the walk, good and bad, and handing them to me like a gift to be cherished for the rest of my life.

Dick waited for me at the foot of the hill and we crossed the stream and climbed the hillside to the bothy whose red roof we had seen from afar. I was quickly brought down to earth; you're never sure who you're going to find in a bothy or how it's going to be, and it's not to be expected that everybody occupying one of these open shelters will have the same standards of usage, for example some people find it impossible to conceive that the refuse collectors don't call every week, or that there's nobody to do the tidying up, and no refrigerator.

It looked as though the rubbish collectors had been and emptied a dustbin on the floor; there were empty or half–used food and drink cans everywhere. The fireplace was choked with ashes and charred incombustible materials and the floor covered with cigarette ends and other rubbish. There was a pile of tins and packets of uneaten food, some of it perishable. These visitors must have had more money than was good for them, I thought; in my youth I was just too poor and hungry to discard food in such a cavalier way.

We set about clearing up, dug a pit to bury what couldn't be burned, and got a fire going to consume the rest, swept the floor and made the place habitable. The bothy code suggests you try to leave the place better than you find it; in one bothy, I can't remember which, somebody has suggested that if everyone were to do this there would soon be heaven on earth!

198

July 5th: I'd thought I would be too excited to sleep on the hard floor but even the noise of the mouse rooting around the fireplace didn't keep me awake for long. We were still up and about by six–thirty, the earliest rising of the whole walk, and away by seven–thirty to follow the tiny path to Sandwood Loch. One route from here continues along the coast to Cape Wrath, but we'd decided to strike inland, staying high. Leaving the lochside path for our final encounter with trackless waste we climbed the steep hillside, knowing we just needed to follow our noses north. We had seen no one since leaving the road yesterday and in the peace and solitude of this early morning we might have been the only people on an unspoiled new earth.

We descended into Strath Chailleach, with a deserted bothy at its head, and crossed a river which flowed down the strath to the sea far below. The coastline was now in view stretching ahead but Cape Wrath still tantalisingly out of sight. The way went on over a series of low rises rather like the peat moorlands, with the coast unrolling to our left. After miles of boggy tussocks we climbed the hill from Loch Keisgaig and came on to firmer ground with its sandstone bones laid bare. The view unfolded to our right, more hills and beyond them the blue sea.

After a while we came to the tip of a great prow of land where through a trick of the topography the immediate foreground was hidden, and all that we could see was the sea on three sides stretching away to the far horizon; nothing to suggest that somewhere ahead was Cape Wrath. It could have been the edge of the world; if we took one step from the bare rock on which we stood we would be transported into another universe, the ultima thule which the old explorers thought lay at the limit of discovery. Back in the comfort of home I turned up Keats' magic words:

> *Then felt I like some watcher of the skies*
> *When a new planet swims into his ken;*
> *Or like stout Cortez when with eagle eyes*
> *He star'd at the Pacific – and all his men*
> *Looked at each other with a wild surmise –*
> *Silent, upon a peak in Darien.*

Only a few yards further and the illusion was gone; the ground fell away in folds, with patches of bare white rock and, lower, peat hags looking as if they would need our careful attention. A deep stream cut a chasm towards the coastal cliffs. Far away to the front the ground rose again, and just below the skyline a Dinky toy of a vehicle was making its way: the Cape Wrath minibus, such a strange intrusion on this wild landscape. We were still more than an hour's walking away.

We made our way down the slope, crossed the stream and climbed again to where the road took a sweeping curve towards Cape Wrath. It wasn't much of a highway, more like some of the estate roads we had walked along; it seemed appropriate that it should be so. Just a few yards further we turned a corner and there was the lighthouse ahead. The time was three-fifteen.

There isn't a great deal to see at Cape Wrath: a lighthouse, some white buildings, and a tiny visitor centre; there was no reception committee either, just a few summer visitors wandering around. It wasn't really too different from Beachy Head – except for the miles between.

I walked onto the headland for photographs, and looked out to the empty sea. The Norsemen gave Cape Wrath its name: turning point. Here I would turn and head for home. I began to realise that it was over; I had no further to walk.

We talked to a young woman with a party about to start out for Sandwood and told her I had walked from Beachy Head; she said, 'Oh how marvellous', and 'I would love to do something like that.' The minibus came and people appeared from different directions to board it. The driver said, 'You made it then?' and charged us seven pounds for the ten-mile bone-shaking drive to the Durness ferry.

18: Aftermath

It's more than a mile from the Cape Wrath ferry into Durness, a distance we didn't feel we needed to walk, so we looked hopefully towards a couple with a dog getting into their estate car and were rewarded with the offer of a lift.

We collected our spare gear from the hotel where we'd left it with Mrs Mackay, and pitched the tent on the local camp site, a large scenic one looking out to sea with a view to Whiten Head, which we recognised from previous visits to the North coast. The school holidays had just started so there had been a population explosion in Durness, and the campsite was crowded with caravans and motorhomes, many with foreign number–plates. After days of solitude we felt bemused to be once more among what seemed like crowds of people.

What we wanted most, after showers and change of clothes was food, but by the time we got round to looking for it Durness's temperance hotel had stopped serving. There is a restaurant on the campsite, which we entered briefly, only to be repelled by excessive noise and tobacco fumes. Cheated of a celebration meal, we dined on a half–packet of soup, dried egg cooked without fat, and a packet of Smash, all the provisions we had left and went to bed without even the solace of a dram, our supply of Scotch having run out.

The Atlantic depression which we had seen coming blew up in the night, a fierce wind from the west and driving rain. We packed up a wet tent and waited for the daily bus outside the general store. The bus was crowded with an assortment of heavily laden backpackers and commuting locals, and took us on a tour of North Sutherland, first the ferry hotel, then around the coast to Kinlochbervie, that amazingly thriving northern fishing port. By the time we reached Scourie the rain had stopped and

201

we abandoned public transport.

Scourie we knew from a previous visit; four years ago we had spent a wet September week camping there. By the end of the week we were the only denizens of the site, everyone else having given the weather best and gone home. We had appreciated the camp–site's outsize tumbler dryer for wet clothes and bedding after one night's storm which flooded the tent.

The friendly Anchorage restaurant was just opening so we had coffee and bacon rolls, then took up position by the roadside to wait for a lift. There wasn't much traffic, a car about every five minutes, but the lift came in the end, a schoolteacher on touring holiday; she had wondered about going to Lochinver, she said, but Ullapool would do just as well, and within the hour we had driven the forty miles to Ullapool and were recovering the car.

We picked up our own hitch–hiker to take to Braemore Junction, stopped on the Dirrie More for lunch, and by evening were booking in at B&B in Newtonmore on the edge of the Cairngorms. We had our postponed celebration meal in the Glen Hotel, and another the next evening, with Audrey and John in Derby.

Driving home along the length of Scotland and England took us two days compared with the hundred it had taken me to walk over a thousand miles; we drove through the changing landscape, from the bare treeless slopes of the far north to wide fields dappled with poppies and full of ripening cereal crops getting ready for harvest. The verges of the roads were lush green and the trees were heavy with summer leaves. We crossed the Clyde and Forth Canal, and, much further south, the place where I'd crossed the M6 in the Midlands. I kept telling myself that I'd walked every step of the way.

Returning home was a repeat of last year, but different too, because I had completed the unfinished business, and I felt that sadness which must always go with endings, however wished–for in their outcome. I had to find a way of weaving the experiences of the walk into the fabric of my life then putting them behind me. There was an immediate strong need to find another challenge; I felt I couldn't settle until I had found one. So I talked Dick into entering with me for the 1993 Great Outdoors

Challenge.

This is a coast-to-coast walk across the 'thick' part of Scotland. Each May two hundred and fifty walkers set out from one of ten points on the west coast to walk to Montrose on the east coast within a time limit of two weeks. The challenge can be made more sporting if you wish by climbing some high mountains on the way. I thought I would feel quite content without such added obstacles.

So we did the Challenge, in rough weather, and by the time we arrived in Montrose my Hawkins boots which had taken me from Derby to Cape Wrath were coming apart and would do no more walking. I couldn't bear to throw them away, so, planted with geraniums they rest on our front porch.

Somehow doing the Challenge enabled me to package my long walk so that it became a part and not the whole of my life; after Cape Wrath there were other things to do and be.

One enduring theme that remains is that of change: since I first found my way around the Derbyshire hills, the world, the countryside and I have all changed – perhaps myself most of all. After all, as the man said, I'm no longer a young woman, and over the years hills become steeper and roads longer. Inside, of course, the feelings are the same.

These feelings are about the joy to be gained from going out into the open air, from learning respect for wildlife and places and people, from experiencing all kinds of weather and from watching the turn of the seasons; there is the satisfied fatigue which comes from the end of a day's walk. There is the confidence of having and using skills of navigation with map and compass, and in judgment of changes of weather and terrain. There are the lifelong friendships of others sharing the love of walking, and above all there is the rich hoard of memories sufficient for a lifetime. All these treasures can be found in plenty in our bountiful British Isles; in North Scotland, if that is your preference, but equally a few miles from your own front door, wherever that may be.

As for me, I'm recognising a familiar hunger, the one which took me to Beachy Head and was only partially satisfied by arriving at Cape Wrath. Somewhere simmering on the back burner are the ingredients of another long walk; one that would start on the east coast where East Anglia reaches out into the North Sea, and finish on one of the Welsh headlands looking out to the Irish Sea. By 1998, which will see my seventy–fifth birthday, I should be ready to start.

'For there is good news yet to hear, and fine things to be seen
Before we go to Paradise by way of Kensal Green.'

Sandwood Bay and Cape Wrath

Appendix: Some facts and figures.

To get from Beachy Head to Newcastleton I walked six hundred and twenty–three miles, and from Newcastleton to Cape Wrath four hundred and thirty–six miles, a total of one thousand and fifty–nine miles in all, and probably about two hundred and fifty miles further than I could have walked in a direct line, if that had been possible. The route was chosen more for its variety than for any wish that it should be direct. Time taken was one hundred days, with twelve rest days added on. Miles per day averaged eleven and a half in England and ten in Scotland, with the daily average getting progressively lower as I moved north. The longest day's walk was twenty–four miles, from Newcastleton to Hawick and the shortest two and a half miles, from Marsden to Forest Farm.

The British Isles are crooked, but they are also lumpy; an end–to–end walk necessarily involves climbing and descending numbers of these lumps, even if no deliberate diversions are made for the purpose of hill–climbing. The amount of feet ascended tends to be increased if the route is mainly off–road, and in a walk of a thousand miles it is quite possible to clock up the number of vertical feet to a total of Himalayan dimensions. In the hundred miles of the South Downs Way from Beachy Head to Winchester, for example, the highest point is the 813 feet of Ditchling Beacon, while the total ascent is about seven thousand feet, which if repeated over a thousand miles would bring the climbing to seventy thousand feet, that is two and a bit Everests!

For maps I used the Ordnance Survey Landranger 1.50,000 series, supplemented by the Peak District and Cotswold Tourist maps but I don't really get on with one–inch maps any more, and hardly used the latter. I got through twentyone maps for the

English section and eighteen for the Scottish. Along with guides, route description and accommodation lists, these were among the weightier items of my baggage and I was glad to have points along the way where I could discard the used ones and collect the batch for the next stage of the walk.

(As an aside, although Britain as a member of the European Union has been committed to metrication for more than twenty years, there is some reluctance to put this commitment into practice; OS Landranger maps all use metric heights, but the Ordnance Survey still print one–inch Tourist maps, and our road and footpath signs cling determinedly to miles rather than kilometres. Readers will find this ambivalence reflected throughout this book, where I freely range between feet and metres; I make no apologies.).

Crossing county boundaries came to be experienced as notable events, in England at least, and I crossed sixteen of these in all including the final border crossing into Scotland. After that I think I was more interested in moving from one kind of terrain to another; the contrast between, say, the countryside of the Scottish Lowlands and that of the Highlands, produces its own definition of territory without the need to observe county boundaries. But one of the great excitements of the walk was in observing the unrolling of the scenery as I moved on.

Looking back in the light of the very wet and stormy conditions which plagued Scotland throughout the autumn and winter of 1992 I realise how very fortunate I was in the weather. In England I had no rain For the first fourteen days; thereafter it rained on thirty–three of the remaining forty–six days, which seems rather a lot but,didn't seem too bad at the time.

In Scotland the first twenty–seven days were fine and mostly hot, after a very wet spring. Besides the greater comfort afforded by walking in the dry, I benefited enormously in the low state of the rivers in the more northerly sections. After Tomdoun there was an unsettled spell which persisted throughout the crossing to Dundonnell. From Ullapool we were blessed with cool but mostly fine conditions, with sunshine and northerly winds for the final vital section to Cape Wrath.

Most of the equipment I needed for the walk I already

possessed. My five–year–old Karrimor Lynx rucksack needed repair at Kirkland after a pocket holding the internal frame collapsed and gave me an uncomfortable time for a few days until I realised what was causing the trouble. I had no other problems with equipment, most of it tried and tested. My two pairs of boots, the Brasher boots used for the southern end of the walk, and my Hawkins Hillwalkers, gave sterling service and I completed the whole walk without a single blister. The Softie sleeping bag I bought in Fort William was exactly right for the conditions in weight and warmth.

For the camping stages Caroline lent her Trangia cooker, which I unreservingly found the best of any camping stoves I had ever used; Caroline also lent the much–abused Ultimate brand tent, which performed admirably even without the added convenience of pegs.

The use of B&B accommodation wherever possible meant that for much of the walk I was able to travel light, and until Fort William the weight I carried rarely exceeded fifteen pounds; I unashamedly allowed Caroline and, later, Dick to carry the heaviest of the camping gear for the final stages of the walk.

For walking I wore a pair of light polycotton trousers with multiple pockets and zips, which were immensely comfortable, drying almost instantaneously, so much so that I was able to dispense with waterproof trousers. By the time I reached Kirkland my twenty–year old cotton shirt was in danger of falling to pieces and I had to replace it with a slightly newer one bought second–hand from Flip in Covent Garden. [Scotland, even in summer, demands sturdier gear, and I changed to a Viyella shirt and heavier sweater.] In England during the dry weather of the first two weeks I carried a light nylon proofed waterproof, exchanging it at Cheltenham for my Berghaus Goretex jacket which served as both waterproof and windproof and was with me for the rest of the walk. For emergencies I carried a Helly Hansen thermal shirt and a light sweater which doubled for evening wear along with a pair of lightweight cotton trousers and a short–sleeved shirt.

I used an assortment of headgear: setting out from Beachy Head I wore a white Christopher Robin sun–hat, which quickly became redundant in the absence of heat–wave weather and was sent home from Salisbury. Throughout I carried a pull–on wool bobble–hat for warmth when required, together with a thin acrylic balaclava, which was a great comfort worn under a Goretex hood in the wet.

I took to Scotland my special Scottish hat, which accompanies me on every Scottish holiday; made of wool tweed, with a brim to keep off rain, sun, flies and midges, it was inherited from a relative and is cherished for its age and shapelessness as well as its utility.

Unless one's skin is made of leather, it isn't safe to cross the border without carrying midge repellent, but I only made use of my supply on one occasion, on the banks of Loch Lomond – which *has* to be a record.

My luxury item was a light–weight personal radio, which gave me great pleasure as well as being helpful for weather forecasts. I carried a paper–back book throughout, rereading Tolkien's *Lord of the Rings* for the umpteenth time during the first weeks, then starting Wilkie Collins' *The Woman in White*, which I took unfinished to Scotland and read while weatherbound at Lochan Fada.

Food was never much of a problem, although I missed eating home–grown vegetables and home–made bread. I relied upon the large breakfasts at B&Bs to keep me going for most of the day, topped up with fruit and nut chocolate and raisins, and usually managed an evening meal either at my lodgings or in the nearest pub. We tried to travel light for camping and bothying so tended to subsist on dehydrated foods, not too satisfying, but we made up for it once back under a roof.

Having consciously set out carrying as I thought the minimum load, I still found myself shedding surplus gear along the way – and not missing it. When in doubt, leave it out!

Some suggested reading

This is just a short, by no means exhaustive, list of books and guides I found useful in planning and doing the walk, or simply reading about the experience of others. Not all of the books are still in print and some have been reprinted many times so I have not included publication dates. For up-to-date information on long-distance paths I recommend the *Long Distance Walker's Handbook* 5th Edition by Barbara Blatchford [Black 1994]

Andrew Ken, *Southern Upland Way* Countryside Commission
Bennet Donald [Ed], *The Munros* Scottish MC
Brown Hamish, *Hamish's Mountain Walk* Paladin; *Hamish's Groats End Walk* Paladin; *Scotland Coast to Coast* Stephens
Haddon, J., Portrait of Bath Hale
Hillaby, John, *Journey Through Britain* World Books
Jebb, Miles,*The* South Downs Way Constable
Lewis, J., *Walking the Cotswold Way* David and Charles
Marriott, M ., *The Footpaths of Britain* Queen Anne Press
Main, Laurence, *A Wiltshire Way* Thornhill Press
McInnes, J. and K., *Walking Through Scotland*
Merrill, John, *Turn Right at Land's End* Oxford Ill. Press
Moir, D.G., *Scottish Hill Tracks No2* Bartholomew
Neillands, R., *The Road to Compostella* Moorland
Reynolds, Kev, *The South Downs Way and the Downs Link* Cicerone
Richards, M., *The Cotswold Way* Harmondsworth
Speakman, Colin, *The Dales Way* Dalesman Books
Tracy, H., *The Heart of England Way* Hamish Hamilton
Vernon, T., *Fat Man on a Roman Road* Michael Joseph
Wainwright, A., *Pennine Way Companion* Westmorland Gazette
West Highland Way Official Guide HMSO
White, H.P., *Forgotten Railways* David and Charles

INDEX